This booklet contains extracts from:

FOOTBALL
CONFIDENTIAL 1

IAN BENT, RICHARD McILROY
KEVIN MOUSLEY

FOOTBALL
CONFIDENTIAL 2

DAVID CONN, CHRIS GREEN,
RICHARD McILROY & KEVIN MOUSLEY

BBC
BOOKS

This booklet contains extracts from:
Football Confidential, first published in 2000
(paperback), and *Football Confidential 2*,
first published in 2003 (paperback).

This promotional compilation was specially
created for *FourFourTwo* by
BBC Books, BBC Worldwide Ltd
Woodlands, 80 Wood Lane, London, W12 0TT

Football Confidential was first published in
paperback in 2000
© Ian Bent, Richard McIlroy, Kevin Mousley
and Peter Walsh 1999
Football Confidential 2 was first published in
paperback in 2003
© David Conn, Chris Green, Richard McIlroy
and Kevin Mousley 2003
The moral right of the authors has been
asserted.

ISBN 0 563 55149 6 (*Football Confidential*)
ISBN 0 563 48858 1 (*Football Confidential 2*)
ISBN 0 563 52202 X (this compilation)

Contents

CHAPTER ONE

Hunting the Hooligans
With the Undercover Police at France 98

Ten days before the start of the 1998 World Cup finals, a group of men in expensive but casual designer clothes meet at a secret location in the English Midlands. They are veterans of violent disorder at scores of football grounds and are plotting a trip to France. They decide the logistics of their travel and accommodation, choosing hotels outside city centres to avoid detection, discussing which hooligan leaders they are likely to meet, speculating which games are most likely to spark aggro. They have little chance of enjoying the hospitality and unique atmosphere of a great sporting event. They are not going for the football; they're going for the trouble.

The men are Football Intelligence Officers (FIOs), known colloquially as 'spotters', and their meeting place is a high-security police station in Nottingham. They have been chosen – in a selection process every bit as tense as Glen Hoddle's choice for his England squad – to form an élite team to travel to France. There, they will help the *gendarmerie* meet the threat posed by the world's worst soccer thugs.

Most are detective constables hand-picked from the ranks of England's county and metropolitan forces. Week in, week out, they gather information about hooligan gangs which they then use to prevent fights and build evidence. Often their work goes unseen.

'Sometimes we go back to the police commander at the end of the day and he'll say, "Well, nothing happened, that was a nice quiet day". And then we explain that something *was* planned but it was all averted by our policing operation,' says one of them.

'We first sent Football Intelligence Officers abroad as spotters in 1990 for the World Cup,' says assistant Chief Constable Tim Hollis, the man responsible for the policing of football in England and Wales. 'Since then we've built up a team of international spotters, local FIOs with their own forces, who have developed a level of expertise and knowledge of fans who cause disorder on a wider scale.'

At Nottingham, the all-male team was briefed by Detective Chief Superintendent Eddie Curtis, who would lead them in France. He was chosen partly because of his wide policing experience – including the violent disorder of the Miners' Strike in the early 1980s – and partly because he speaks fluent French. Given the proximity of the tournament – a short trip through the Channel Tunnel – and the presence of other clubs with active hooligans such as Germany, Holland, Belgium, Italy and Argentina, he knew he was likely to be under considerable pressure, but his manner was relaxed and jokey.

There would be a lot riding on the spotters and some were feeling the strain. One detective constable with a key intelligence-collating role confided that he couldn't sleep for a week before the tournament because of 'worry and stress'.

For all of them, though, the trip was a career peak. The oldest member of the team was Jack, a weathered, pipe-smoking northerner who turned down a professional rugby league offer to join the police. Now, just months away from retirement, France 98 was to be the icing on the cake. 'It has to be the top, hasn't it? Most FIOs would give their right arms to be in the position that we are. I've been looking forward to it from the day I got the telephone call to say I was going.'

Jack normally policed a lower-division club with a relatively small following. His typical Saturday duty would be crowd control at some wind-blown Third Division outpost. He was selected for France because of the notoriety of their active hooligan element.

'Although we are a small club, they are big contenders on the England scene for the international hooligan. They're well-known throughout the hooligan world. They go abroad a lot, and quite a few of them have been arrested abroad and deported.'

Although they wear plain clothes abroad, at home the spotters work in uniform, filming crowds or speaking to fans at games. They gather titbits from informants and other sources and phone each other before games to swap knowledge and draw up a match-day plan. Bill, from a Midlands force, has been trailing the thugs for 15 years and once spent months undercover infiltrating a particularly violent gang.

'It's a cat-and-mouse game. We're the cats – and I've never yet seen a mouse eat a cat. You follow the intelligence as it is occurring – normally by the minute – and just follow your nose, follow your instinct. It's like a hunt.'

Such is the secrecy of their work that, until permission was given for *On The Line* to follow the team in France, no media organization had ever been allowed to accompany the international spotters on duty.

What follows is a unique insider's account of what happened there. Restrictions on revealing the names and number of the spotters have been respected. Otherwise this is the unvarnished diary of France 98: the Spotters' Story.

Saturday, 13 June

Most of the spotting team fly to Marseilles, the host city for England's first game against Tunisia. No sooner have they landed than they are out on the streets, helping the French police to deal with a disturbance in the Old Port area, where several hundred England fans are drinking. Trouble flares again at the end of the night when a British fan falls off a car and is hit by another vehicle. Policing is complicated by factors beyond the spotters' control: the second biggest city in France has a high crime rate, a tough reputation and simmering racial tensions among its large North African immigrant community.

Sunday, 14 June

The FA's security adviser, Sir Brian Hayes, plays down the previous night's bother at a well-attended morning press conference. 'I think it's important to keep everything in proportion. It's a big busy town, there was drinking and rowdy behaviour, a few bottles thrown. At the end of the day there were four people arrested. Two have been released. In the general run of things it was a minor incident.'

Down on the narrow Prado beach that afternoon, rival fans mingled peacefully in the sunshine beside a giant TV screen. There was little hint of what was to follow – what one spotter called 'the worst violence I have ever witnessed'.

By early evening a boozy English hard core was massing at a waterfront bar called O'Malleys. Some then left the pub and tried to burn an Irish flag before chanting, 'No Surrender to the IRA'. That soon turned to, 'Come on, let's do the Old Bill'.

A spotter takes up the story. 'We and a French police officer decided to try and identify certain people up there.

We were in amongst them when they recognized that we were police officers and suddenly wanted to attack us. Perhaps not having the guts to do it physically they started chucking bottles and all sorts of things at us. We were chased, stoned and bottled and had to make a tactical retreat ... but if we hadn't done that some of us might not be here to tell the tale.'

A volley of tear-gas stopped the pursuing louts in their tracks. Noxious clouds drifted through Marseilles' restaurant quarter, leaving innocent diners spluttering into their shellfish. It was to be the first of many barrages that evening.

Dressed in civvies, the spotters had no visible means of identifying themselves and, despite their French 'minders', were sometimes mistaken for hooligans by the heavily-armed riot police. 'At one stage the French police thought they were English hooligans, the local youths thought they were English hooligans, and English hooligans knew they were spotters,' said Eddie Curtis, 'so they came under attack from all three sides.'

A forty-yard no man's land opened up between the riot squad in helmets, shields and body armour and the English fans in shorts and polo shirts. Some of the hooligans picked up chairs, bottles and sticks and hurled them at the police lines. One of the dozens of press cameramen swarming around like mosquitoes ventured too close; he was punched, kicked and chased off.

The attitude of the French police, who simply stood their ground, firing tear-gas when the hooligans got too close, bemused their English colleagues. There was little attempt to disperse the fans or to make arrests. Still, it gave the English team plenty of opportunities to video the ensuing riot with their hand-held cameras.

Finally, after two hours of tear-gas and taunts that would be shown on news broadcasts around the world, the police made their move, marching forward in a line and banging their shields like Zulus. The hooligans tried to gee each other up to stand their ground but when the police broke into a charge the fans fled, leaving broken windows and an overturned car in their wake.

Meanwhile, on the other side of the harbour, scores of Arab youths and some of Marseilles' own soccer hooligans engaged in a pitched battle with a small group of English. The ground was soon littered with broken glass. Anyone caught alone was brutally beaten. One man was trapped down a side street and his throat was cut. Several of the spotters and a plain-clothes French colleague were caught up in the terror.

'We were with a father and son from Leeds who were terrified and we were trying to get them to safety. There was panic when tear-gas was fired at the crowd and we ran into an alley to get away. We were confronted by thirty to forty French youths. They thought we were English football supporters. It was very dangerous. I thought we were going to get stabbed.

'Then the French police officer pulled out his ID. They backed off but you could tell they were frustrated. They said to us, "You tell the English hooligans, the fucking French hooligans are still alive. We are waiting for you". This group then attacked English supporters who were outside a hotel. After this, they moved on to a bar where there were English and attacked that group as well, causing a number of injuries.'

The bar owner and a powerfully-built but terrified bouncer pulled down a metal shutter to keep out local thugs who were trying to smash their way in to attack the

English. By midnight, the darkness was split by the blue flashing lights of police vehicles. The acrid tang of tear-gas was everywhere, glass and debris littered the streets. And some of the gangs were still fighting.

'We came upon a number of English supporters who had been stabbed and slashed with knives,' says a London officer. 'A number were saying they were just trying to get back to their hotels. They were almost fighting for their lives. We attempted to move them away but, in our view, it was clear that everywhere they went they were being attacked.'

Monday, 15 June
As Eddie Curtis and his men watched their video evidence the next day, they realized they had spectacular material which would be used repeatedly over the following weeks to arrest and convict the ringleaders. 'After filming this sort of stuff for the past 15 years, that was probably the best evidence I've ever filmed,' said one of the team.

Police forces worldwide grade soccer thugs in to three categories: A, B and C. The worst are Category C, those who organize violence, and Category B, those most likely to join in. There are judged to be about 200 Category Cs on the England international scene.

For the match, Detective Chief Superintendent Curtis split his team into small groups, each tasked with watching a different area of the city, and briefed them on the day's tactics: 'If there's anybody selling tickets on the black market, tell your French colleagues. They're going to lock them up and take their tickets. If we've got any Category Cs and Category Bs on the beach, ask them if they've got tickets.'

Each group then piled into an unmarked Renault Espace people-carrier, driven by the French officers who were their constant companions, and headed off, meeting later at the Stade Velodrome. Their first stop was at a garage, to stock up on chocolate bars: such had been the frenzy of their first 48 hours on foreign soil that few of the spotters had been able to grab a proper meal; one group claimed to have eaten only a large bag of Bombay Mix brought over from the UK.

Inside the Stade Velodrome, their job was to watch the crowd, film some faces with hand-held cameras and try to pick out any people from the disorder the previous night. A valuable source of information were the flags, revealing the names of home towns and clubs, that many England followers display.

There was some sporadic skirmishing outside the ground, but most of the trouble that day occurred by the big screen on the beach after England scored the first of the two goals that would secure them victory. Several innocent people were injured by missiles. The atmosphere that evening was tense, but there were few further clashes as most of the England contingent either left the city or stayed away from the Old Port area. Still, the spotters were out until well after midnight.

Tuesday, 16 June
The spotters' first downtime. After helping to take statements from some of those being held at Marseilles police station, the officers are invited to another station at a small beach near the resort. Lunch was followed by beach volleyball and a spot of sunbathing, the pale white bodies of the English force a comic contrast to the well-tanned locals. Even then, a couple of the group spent the afternoon hunched over a laptop, feeding in information on some of their target 'faces' seen over the weekend.

Although unanimous in their condemnation of the trouble, the spotters were well aware that the majority of England fans in Marseilles had not been involved. 'It's important to put things in perspective,' said one. 'We must have been looking, at a conservative estimate, at 10-15,000 England fans in the stadium. Even at the height of the Sunday night trouble there were only 300 involved, and only a few of these were deliberately provoking disorder, maybe as few as 150. So we are talking about a significantly low figure.'

Not everyone blamed the English. At least one French bar gave free drinks to Brits for fighting with the local Arabs, a reflection of racial antagonism in an area where the right-wing *Front National* is popular. Paris police sergeant Jean Paul Tarot, who was with the English spotters, was objective. 'The world's Press say it's the English, always the English, but in France you have the problem with the French Arabs. The problem was fifty-fifty, not just the English people.'

Some of the spotters head off to Montpelier, where Italy are playing, to check out information that English gangs might be there.

Wednesday–Friday, 17–19 June
Much of the spotters' time was spent on the road, swilling warm bottles of mineral water and listening to tapes of football songs; long periods of *ennui* that contrasted vividly with the adrenaline-pumping excitement of crowd control. The drive from Marseilles to Toulouse took them from a noisy Mediterranean melting pot to a cosmopolitan city of smart cafés and art shops. They were greeted by good-natured groups of fans drinking in the main square, the *Place du Capitole*, and by the news that special powers

had been introduced by the French authorities to allow the immediate expulsion of any Category C thugs.

'The police can detain suspects for four hours, and if we look at their record and see they have a long record of violence, particularly at football matches, we will point that out and the local French prefect will decide if that person can stay,' said Eddie Curtis. 'If he considers that person a danger then he will send him home.'

These new legal powers were just what the spotters had wanted.

Saturday, 20 June
The spotters toured Toulouse with their French colleagues and set up a couple of secret observation points. Little sign of trouble.

Sunday, 21 June
To relieve them of some of the organizational burden, the team was joined by a French-speaking logistics officer from the Metropolitan Police, DCI Kevin Hurley. He briefed them on the new powers at the main police station – where a large armour-plated water-cannon was parked ominously in the forecourt.

'Okay, you are going to be followed around by a plain-clothes arrest team. The idea is for you to identify anyone who is a Category C. We are going to bring them in like before, but then they will go through immediate emergency expulsion. Just say they are Category C, *arrêtez-lui*, and they will. You can all say that, can't you?'

It was to be a day not of arrests however, but of fight-prevention. The first incident happened that afternoon in the café-lined main square, where hundreds of good-natured England fans were milling around. Three local Arab youths took it upon themselves to hurl insults at one group of supporters and, as the English lads walked over to confront them, one of the youths brandished a large stick.

Three of the spotters were filming the incident, but when they realized it could blow up into violence, they quickly called in the French police. Within seconds the local youth was arrested and – probably for the first and only time in their careers – the spotters were treated to a round of applause from the England fans.

The outcome was in stark contrast to events perpetrated the same day by German thugs in the northern French town of Lens; a helmeted and armed gendarme was beaten into a coma with a paving stone. Rumours – which later proved false – circulated that he had died. So when 300 England fans became a nuisance outside a bar called the Melting Pot, dozens of grim-faced CRS riot police in the now-familiar Robocop gear lined up a few hundred yards down the road and prepared to charge.

The spotters were also rushed to the scene. 'There was a problem when the English spilled on to the road,' said one. 'There must have been 100 or more in the road, all of them had been drinking and they were obviously blocking the road. I was wearing the same as the other lads: shorts and T-shirt, but by now we'd been given armbands so the French police would know who we were.'

In a bid to prevent mayhem, the French commander asked DCI Hurley if his men would mediate with the fans and get them to move. Not all of the spotters were happy: they had no protective clothing and no powers of arrest in a foreign country. Still, they fanned out across the dark street and tried to persuade the fans to move. 'Come on lads, keep out of the road now. Let the traffic through!'

While some of the revellers began to move away, others were very drunk and trying to incite the rest to attack the police. A few bottles and glasses were thrown. Not for the first time, the situation was made worse by the presence of photographers and reporters who used the advancing British officers as cover to approach the crowd and take pictures. They, rather than the police, became an immediate target for attack, with the spotters caught in the middle.

Eventually, as the French police marched up in ranks with batons drawn, the spotters were forced to back away. The road was cleared without unnecessary force and, in the event, only one man was arrested, then quickly released after a sobbing protest from his girlfriend. It was another successful and relatively peaceful operation, but not all the officers were happy.

'To be fair, some of the lads thought we were put in an unnecessary situation. With hindsight the operation worked well and we did help the French police, but I don't think any of us would want to be put in that situation again. We definitely felt vulnerable.'

Which was a diplomatic way of saying that some of the spotters were angry at being exposed. There was some plain-speaking that night behind closed doors. Commanding officer Eddie Curtis acknowledged his men's vulnerability, but supported the decision to send them in.

'They certainly did feel exposed. But the person responsible on the ground took a calculated decision that there were not any really nasty people in that crowd who would have been able to whip up violence.'

Monday, 22 June
England v Romania. Kick-off is not until early evening but one of the English police team is at the stadium from noon.

Phil works for the National Criminal Intelligence Service (NCIS), which collates intelligence on serious criminals ranging from gangsters to sex offenders. Football hooligan gangs also fall within its remit.

In a meeting room under one of the stands he sets up a TV set and laptop computer. He has two mobile phones, one to connect his computer to the Internet and the other to field calls from his colleagues out on the streets. As they phone in with sightings of particular faces, he keys the information into a running log and also e-mails the NCIS HQ in London, where they check criminal records and files on Category C targets on a computer system called 'Goalkeeper'.

The laptop and modem are on loan from computer firm Hewlett Packard; neither the Home Office, the FA nor the British police were prepared pay for the electronic hardware that was necessary to support an international intelligence operation. (The spotters even had to buy their own team polo shirts.)

'The lads can ring in to me, I'm in electronic contact with my office back in England and can make various requests. The replies are then sent back to me,' says Phil. 'We have a nice little database including photos of most of our major subjects. I can type in a club and can immediately highlight the Category Cs.'

Phil is to spend ten hours in his underground nerve-centre, keeping the lines of intelligence flowing. He leaves his desk only once – to join the crowd for a rousing version of 'God Save The Queen' just before the kick off. 'It made the hairs stand up on the back of my neck,' he says later.

Despite defeat for England, the atmosphere at the ground is incredibly upbeat and there is no trouble. Later the spotters visit the main train station; scores of Brits are crashed out on the concourse, sleeping off their hangovers. Phil arrives back at his hotel well after midnight. The bar is full of celebrating Romanians who have drunk all the beer.

Tuesday, 23 June

The morning is spent souvenir shopping and sight-seeing in Toulouse. Then it's off on the long drive north to Lens for England's crucial game against Colombia. The tired team now face the longest journey of the trip: two hot days on the road in people- carriers, after a string of long days and late nights in low-rent accommodation (one of the hotels they had been booked into was so bad that the spotters took one look and walked straight out again). It is the natural time for morale to flag. Things are not helped when one of the French police drivers, a woman constable from Paris, decides to go into a massive and inexplicable Gallic huff, a mood that will last until the end of the tournament.

Wednesday, 24 June

Lens is hardly likely to lift spirits. A series of conical slag heaps greets visitors to this dull, provincial mining town which even the bunting and flags cannot brighten. Some of the spotters meet up for an evening beer with Dutch police mates they have worked with on previous trips. They swap stories and black humour.

Thursday, 25 June

Twenty miles from Lens is the bigger and busier city of Lille. With its Channel Tunnel terminal, it is going to be the embarkation point for most of the England fans. Thousands are expected, many without tickets, as this game is the easiest to reach of England's first-round matches. The spotters also have intelligence from colleagues watching at ports and train stations that this fixture is likely to attract the heaviest hooligan groups.

In one Lille bar packed with drinking Brits, the spotters identify two Category C targets. They phone in to check their criminal records; under the new powers, the men can be kicked out of the country if their convictions are serious enough. The problem is that any attempt to enter the bar and grab them could spark a riot.

'The French police wanted to go straight in, but we told them to wait until the men left. Eventually, after two hours, they came out in a group of six. We had checked their previous convictions and established that one of the two could be kicked out of the country. Unfortunately, because they're identical twins, we had to take both back to the police station to ascertain which one was which.'

Their softly-softly approach is well-placed. For, over the next twenty-four hours, Lille is to see a gathering of some of the most formidable hooligans gangs, many of them veterans of hundreds of street brawls.

'These, for want of a better phrase, are the better quality of hooligan,' says one spotter. 'Those in Marseilles and Toulouse were more the English-lads-in-Benidorm type, lads away for their holidays together. Here, there hasn't been the singing in the streets, there are not as many England shirts, not as many flags, and the people seem to be watching the streets rather than watching each other. They're more streetwise. At the first sign of disorder they disperse and re-group later somewhere else. They don't stand there to be picked-off by the police or identified by the TV cameras. It's a hit-and-run mentality.'

All the more worrying, then, to find that the police chief at Lille is not expecting the British spotting team, and had only 45 officers on duty the night before the match –

the number you would expect for an average Saturday night in Hull or Brighton. This leads to a lively debate with DCI Kevin Hurley.

'I've discovered there are no CRS [riot police] or Brigade Gendarmerie Mobil deployed here. They are effectively the public-order police, the men with shields and helmets. I have expressed the view that they might like some on reserve. The French have discussed it and are calling up a company of CRS officers, just under ninety people, to be on standby. I don't think they are aware of the potential difficulties here. They suspect the problems may be in Lens tomorrow.'

The Lille officers, however, do not let their lack of numbers dampen their enthusiasm. By mid-evening the Police Commissariat is filling up with English prisoners, many of them drunk. Each is filmed by the spotters, who also help the French take down their details. Most of the fans are drunk, stroppy and uncooperative.

One particularly offensive trouble-maker takes exception to the possibility that 'They're gonna put us on some fuckin' register'. Despite being handcuffed he lunges across the police car at the spotter who is filming him and has to be restrained by French police. Yet the spotters have found from experience that English hooligans arrested in a foreign country often undergo a remarkable transformation in their attitude to the British police.

'When you're abroad, and they find themselves in police custody and think they may be facing jail, they suddenly become your best friend. They say to you, "Oh, English old Bill, thank God you're here". The same person back home would want to smack you in the mouth. We had one who was arrested for being drunk and wanting to fight the world, but in the back of the car he kept saying,

"I can't take this. My wife will leave me. I'll lose my job," and he was in tears, like a big baby.'

By the end of the night there have been around 50 arrests but no serious trouble.

Friday, 26 June
The spotters split up, some going to Lens, some snooping around Lille train station, others setting up a secret observation post in Lille city centre. From a first-floor office, the men – equipped with binoculars and a video camera – have a bird's-eye view of the soccer gangs which, in the absence of any local opposition, begin to weigh each other up.

'In one small bar we've got confirmed sitings of Wolverhampton and Huddersfield hooligans, a German who has been seen quite a few times with the English, and possibly some Chelsea hooligans,' says Bill. 'There are too many to take anybody out at this time. That would just cause really serious disorder.'

Suddenly a short, sharp fight breaks out between a member of the so-called Newcastle Gremlins gang and a muscular bruiser with no shirt on. It is over almost as soon as it starts, with the out-punched Newcastle fan and his mates moving reluctantly away.

'One small incident like that could start an awful lot of trouble. If the police went in, it would just escalate and probably everyone in the square would get involved in a mass riot.'

There are other minor incidents as some of the rowdier English fans seek to confront the police. Eventually the fans suss out the observation post. They wave and make crude gestures. The spotters decide it is time to go.

Thousands without tickets watch the game that evening on French TV in bars. England win and go through. A ban on booze in Lens contributes to a largely trouble-free night. But one young England follower misses the post-match celebrations when his past crimes catch up with him.

'He was first caught on film throwing bottles towards the police lines in the port area of Marseilles. He didn't just throw one, he threw a box. He was videoed and we made a paste-up on the computer and put him down as "Wanted". We then saw him in Toulouse after we were called to another disturbance, but he noticed us first and ran. On the way he was changing his clothing. We were hoping that we were going to get him in Lens and, sure enough, we went to a small skirmish outside Lens stadium and saw him coming up the road towards us. We informed our French colleagues and they detained him.'

Saturday, 27 June
The spotters show the French police the video evidence they have on the arrested man. Anthony Winstone, from Fulham, is later jailed for four months, the last of the Marseilles riot ringleaders to be caught. It highlights the usefulness of small hand-held cameras – the greatest tools in the spotters' armoury. As Jack explains:

'The hooligans don't like the video camera. They'll do anything to get away from it. They'll cover their heads, wear dark glasses, wear hats, bonnets, collars up, anything. Because once they're on film, if anything goes wrong, they know they can be identified.'

Bill and a colleague once prevented two gangs fighting by standing between them and filming. 'It was like Custer's Last Stand. Two large groups of hooligans were about to attack each other. They started running forward and we found ourselves filming in the middle, working back to back. As the groups ran towards each other they saw us and stopped, almost like a cartoon freeze-frame. It certainly held them off long enough for other officers to arrive and disperse them.'

Sunday, 28 June
Another long journey ahead, up to St Etienne for the second-round tie against Argentina. Plenty of time to discover how boring French radio can be; at least you can pick up Radio 5 Live in places.

Monday, 29 June
A briefing at St Etienne police station. Next to the rather bedraggled English spotters sit a smartly-uniformed three-man contingent from the Argentinian police. A French officer explains at length, with the aid of various charts, his plans for policing and segregation. Unfortunately he speaks entirely in French and none of the spotters understands a word.

Despite media reports suggesting an Argentinian hooligan threat, Eddie Curtis is unconcerned: 'They have 15 of what they call Category Cs, but we only call someone Category C if they actually direct problems. The Argentinians probably categorize people C if they cause trouble or are liable to follow trouble. So a very small number.'

The officers are then taken to the ground to have a look round, but the security staff refuse to let them in.

Tuesday, 30 June
The spotters hang around St Etienne police station for several hours waiting to be given instructions. While there, one of Huddersfield Town's best known 'boys' is brought

in handcuffed. He banters with the spotters about their dress sense, proudly displaying his Burberry hat and Stone Island top.

St Etienne's police commander had promised to flood the streets with hundreds of armed officers and deal promptly with any troublemakers. Inevitably, some innocent fans are caught in the net and arrested. When they realize there are English police officers at the station they appeal for their help to get released.

Inevitably, many guilty parties escape arrest and at the packed stadium that evening there are, for the first time at France 98, clashes inside a ground. Argentina's opening goal from a penalty is the trigger for a small disturbance behind the goal where the majority of English fans are gathered. Some try to cross the seats to attack rival fans. It is not long before similar trouble breaks out at the opposite end, where a small but vociferous number of English are in among the blue-and-white of their opponents.

Yet nothing in the stands is as dramatic as events on the pitch. For once, even the spotters find themselves watching the game more than the crowd.

England's exit sees a few scuffles at the ground and later in the town. Frustratingly for the spotters, three of those involved are Newcastle Category Cs who had earlier been pointed out to the French police, arrested but then released.

Wednesday, 1 July
A mixture of sadness and relief. All of the spotters, football fans themselves, wanted England to do well. But by now they are also tired and missing their families. Enough is enough.

With the pressure off, a game of soccer is organized against some local firemen. It is a time to unwind and, for Eddie Curtis, to look back at the past two-and-a-half weeks.

'It has gone very well. We had a strategy. We said we would point out the people who were liable to cause trouble, gather evidence on those who did cause trouble and advise the local police accordingly, and we did. The local police said they would deal with people swiftly and take them before the court, and they did. They said they would deal with them severely and give terms of imprisonment, and they did. Everybody has shown tremendous courage in some very difficult situations.'

The spotters themselves are left with indelible memories.

'It has been a marvellous experience, something I will never forget,' says one. 'Some of the situations we dealt with we have never had to deal with before. For example, I've been involved in disorder on a grand scale but never on such a scale as in Marseilles.'

For others, it is the end of an era. A third of the team who travelled to France are to leave soccer intelligence for other duties. Bill, after 15 years tracking headline-grabbing gangs, is on his way to a motorized beat in a rural English county. He admits that he might miss the hooligans.

'I think I will in a way. It has been a pleasure to stop them causing problems over the years. It'll be very difficult watching a football match after doing this job. If I go on my day off, I'll end up talking to people I know and not watching the game. Even when I watch it on TV, I look at the crowd – who's there? – I just can't help it. You become addicted.'

CHAPTER TWO

Sorted!

Why Drug Tests in English Football Help to Paint a False Picture of Drug Abuse Within the Game

The FA claim their drugs testing system is the most comprehensive for any sport in this country. In fact it is so ineffective that a player would have to play for over 400 years before having half a chance of being tested. Footballers have the means, the motive and the expertise at their disposal to take advantage of the finest performance enhancing drugs. In ten years of Premiership football not one first team player has been caught using any drug of any description. And as things stand, they are not likely to.

In the past decade and a half there are few sports that have not experienced the fallout of a positive drugs test. Runners, jumpers, throwers, cyclists, weightlifters, rugby players, swimmers and the rest have all at one time or another hit the headlines as a result of performers popping pills they ought not to have popped. Specifically pills that aid performance, so-called performance enhancing drugs.

Odd then, isn't it, that even though athletes from almost any sport you care to name have been done, in by far the biggest sport in the country – football – there is yet to be a positive test for a performance enhancing drug. Even though it tests more people than any other sport football is, according to the testers, as clean as a whistle. Every now and then there's bit of marijuana, ecstasy or even heroin but of performance enhancing substances, not a trace.

Do the drugs not work with football? Are footballers naturally squeamish when it comes to taking them? Or is it that the system set up to catch them has so many opt-outs and caveats that a player would have to be monumentally unlucky or staggeringly stupid to get caught? It is a rhetorical question, of course!

In the ten or eleven months of a year that football clubs are in business there are some players who have more reason to loathe Mondays than others. It is the day, custom would have it, that the doping doctors, if they are coming at all, arrive at the training ground.

When they do turn up it works like this. They report to training ground reception or, if it is match day, the stadium. Dr Richard Higgins, club doctor for Sheffield Wednesday, knows the score:

> They turn up unannounced and as I come off the pitch I am told two players have been selected for a drugs test. There is a room at the stadium and training ground set aside for the purpose and the players are taken straight there without being allowed to go into the changing room. They stay there for however long it takes to give a sample.

(This can sometimes be quite a while as footballers are generally pretty dehydrated after running around for a couple of hours.)

In the nine years up to August 2002 since the Premier League was launched there have been 3,465 matches featuring getting on for 2,000 players, but so far there has yet to be a single positive test indicating the use of a performance enhancing drug.

Dr Higgins does not find this odd. He believes British players just don't go for it: 'I have difficulty even convincing the players to take a complex carbohydrate drink because the mentality in the British game is that you don't take supplements. We still have to convince players that drinking tea at half time is a bad idea!' (It makes you wee and causes you to dehydrate alarmingly during exercise.)

The perception within the game is that there is no problem with enhancers but there is a bit of a problem with inhibitors – booze and the so-called recreational drugs. And it is these that most concern the Football Association. Michele Verroken, the drugs control officer at the Sports Council, who runs the programme on behalf of the FA, explains:

> We have noted the prevalence of socially abused drugs. It has been worthwhile to target that area and say, look, there is a zero tolerance towards these substances by the FA so don't waste people's time, money and your careers by using these substances because there is a high chance you will be caught.

Actually, there is not. There have been 62 positive tests for recreational drugs in 14 years. And, it bears repeating, none at all for performance enhancers since the Premier League was launched. They have only ever caught one player over the driving limit for alcohol. Not a good strike rate given the reputation of footballers, and the scope of the testing, which not only covers the four professional leagues but also the reserve, youth and academy leagues and the women's Premier League. During the 1999–2000 season the FA carried out 1,066 tests in and out of competition (match day and training grounds).

They visited 32 matches and 261 training sessions, which breaks down in theory to an average of two visits by a tester in a season. Not that it works out like that in practice, as the youth coach at a professional club in the Midlands told *On The Line*:

> We always give out the FA's information on drugs and what have you and lecture the players on the damage drugs can do, particularly the younger ones. We tell them about testing but I have to say in the seven years I have been here I have never seen a tester.

By contrast, a London club was visited 14 times in 1998. According to popular anecdote, Premier League clubs get at least one visit a season at the training ground but as far as match days go it is a different story.

The 32 matches visited by testers in the 1999–2000 season represented less than 1 per cent of the 3,500-plus league games played that were subject to testing. Factor in the rule that on each visit two players from each side have to give samples and statistically you would have to play professional football for 432 years in England before having a 50–50 chance of being tested at a match.

Greg Moon is a professional drugs tester and he works for the World Anti-Doping Commission (WADA). It is an arm of the International Olympic Committee and Moon and his colleagues are charged with keeping tabs on Olympians all over the world and, when they feel like it, they test them. He thinks the football testing in England is pretty weedy:

> If a club is done one match a year they can pretty much rely that once the test is out of the way they can go along on their merry way regardless. The way to catch people is randomness. Appearing one day

and then very shortly afterwards to catch people with their guard down. Thirty matches does not seem like a very big sample to me and one in which you could have reasonable confidence of avoiding a drugs test, certainly if the testers have been early in the season.

Not only do footballers run an extremely low risk of being tested in the first place but, as I mentioned earlier, it seems that as far as training ground visits go, players are pretty confident about which day of the week the tester will pitch up. One club even gave the dope tester his own parking space before the good doctor realized what an early warning message he was sending out!

Matt Yates, the former international middle distance runner, who now works as a part-time fitness consultant with a number of football clubs, finds the situation risible:

I do know it is a standard joke in football that the testers will be in on Monday morning because they would be looking for social drugs that expensive footballers might have been consuming on the weekend. But that is the least of it; the testing in football is pretty much a joke.

The thinking behind the Monday morning visit is that a drug like cocaine can be out of your system inside three days so Monday is the last chance to catch a Saturday night user. But the players know this and if they have indulged it is easy for them to avoid Monday morning training, reporting in sick, or perhaps indulging their habit midweek when they know there is little chance of being asked to give a sample.

Little wonder then that a doctor told a contact of *On The Line*, 'They always seem to know when I am coming.'

So not only hardly ever and not quite unannounced but also football has managed to negotiate another 'get out' – no home visits for random testing. Indeed, no testing of any kind outside the club's training ground and the stadium on match day. Compare and contrast this with the experience of an athlete like Yates:

> I have sort of semi-retired but even I still get tested. In my career I imagine I was asked to give a sample on around 100 occasions. Typically the phone would go and they would say they were parked around the corner, could they come and do a test? It could be especially intense in the run-up to a major event like the Olympics or a European championship. Basically, the British Olympic Association did not want the embarrassment of being caught out with a doped athlete in the full glare of competition.

You get the impression that Michele Verroken would love to run a similar system within football but the reality is that she knows the clubs would not wear it:

> The present situation is that we do work in partnership with the sports but that does make us reliant upon them to want to participate in the ultimate aim. Admittedly one cynical view may be that some sports are guiding us away from where we should be looking.

Because the FA are not obliged to test for drugs – or opt into the UK Sport programme, the Sports Council have little choice but to negotiate terms. Football has the upper hand here because it does not receive any grants from the Sports Council.

Effectively it is a compromise between best practice and what the clubs will put up with. And what they won't put up with is the prospect of their expensive assets being knocked up in the middle of the night and being asked to wee into a sample bottle.

Howard Wells has worked in professional football at Watford and Ipswich and used to be chief executive of the UK Sports Council. He explains that football is not alone in being able to negotiate opt-outs:

> I think the protocols range from one sport to the other and while we may think there are standard procedures, there are not, and there is a considerable amount of integrity placed on the governing bodies to determine their own rules. Therein lies the problem.

In yet another of its arrangements with football, the matches to be visited by the drugs testers are agreed with the FA before the season kicks off. *On The Line* were unable to find out how much notice the individual clubs get, if any, of an impending visit because neither the FA nor the clubs that we asked would tell us. But at the very least, a precise programme of testing agreed up to nine months in advance would seem to further compromise the all-important unannounced element of a dope test.

On The Line asked WADA's Greg Moon for his opinion about the various opt-outs relating to football and drugs tests:

Well that is just worthless. You might as well not bother going. My definition of 'unannounced' is that you are sitting at home, I knock on your door and it is now. It is not 'Oh, can you come back tomorrow?' It is now. And if they happen to be going to the airport, then I will arrange to go with them and if they get on the plane, I arrange for someone to meet them at the other end.'

As nothing like this ever happens in football you have to treat the FA's assessment of its programme as the most comprehensive in British sport with caution if not scepticism. Football may have doubled the number of tests from 500 to over 1,000 between seasons 1998–9 and 1999–2000 but then it is our biggest sport and compared to the 796 tests carried out in 1999 on athletics in the UK there are massive windows of opportunity for drugs cheats to avoid or prepare for tests.

Frankly, clubs cannot afford to have their star players being caught for using drugs. Unlike many sports subject to dope tests, a positive result in football would have ramifications far beyond the individual player – it could have a catastrophic impact on the team, as Verroken acknowledges: 'It is a liability on their assets. These players are assets to the club but what we try and do is encourage them to be open in their accounting of the testing programme.'

We already know that no player has been done for performance enhancing substances in the last ten years but no *first* team player in the Premier League has ever been positively tested for a recreational drug either.

The majority of the miscreants paraded before the FA disciplinary committee for drugs offences are youth team players or women. The others are all from the lower leagues. Between 1994 and 1999, for example, the clubs involved were West Brom, Reading, Tranmere, Leyton Orient, Huddersfield, Barnsley, Ipswich and Charlton, at a time when these last three teams were not in the Premiership. The only team in the top flight to suffer the embarrassment of a positive test was Newcastle and then the player in question was a youth. The only two high profile players ever to have tested positive (both for marijuana) were Lee Bowyer and Chris Armstrong, and that was at a time when neither was playing in the Premier League.

The fact is that the tabloids have a better record for uncovering drug and alcohol abuse in football than the FA does. Football clubs have every reason to want to wash their dirty linen in private, of course, and there is evidence that some are doing just that, much to the irritation of Verroken:

> It has been reported to us that private testing is going on and all I can do is warn clubs that they have to be absolutely sure that first of all these methods are as effective as the screening methods we use. It is difficult to gauge how widespread private testing is. There are a number of highly successful companies out there and so someone is making money.

It is possible that when players undergo these tests they believe they are sanctioned by the FA. This came to light when a regular England international claimed in an interview with a football magazine in 1999 that he must be the most tested player in Britain and he had no idea that he was spilling any beans.

When they read this at the Euston HQ of UK Sport it was of keen interest because they knew they had never tested him. It must have been someone else. Someone else like the company that wrote to Howard Wells when he was chief executive at Watford during their spell in the Premier League: 'I received a letter from a commercial operation offering services to drugs test our players, which I realized was in conflict with the work being done by UK Sport.'

Howard would have been especially conscious of this because he had left the chief executive's post at UK Sport to take up his job at Watford. How many other clubs received similar letters and what they did with them can only be guessed at. Wells forwarded his letter to the FA but heard no more about it.

Clubs are clearly aware that banned drugs are being passed around dressing rooms or being taken in treatment rooms, on or off their premises, and they would rather find out in private than have their highly prized assets dragged through the press. What makes this all the more galling is that you and I, the taxpayer, help fund this malarkey.

The agreement to allow testing to happen in professional football is that the Sports Council, i.e. the public, pays for the first 250 tests every year. With each test and its associated costs now running at over £500 a pop, which amounts to £100,000 of public money subsidizing drugs tests to little effect in Britain's biggest and richest sport.

On The Line contacted the FA for comment on the drugs issue in football. PR supremo at Soho Square, Paul Newman, said they were 'totally relaxed' over the prospect of any criticism of the FA's drug policy and saw no reason why they should enter into a dialogue with us about it.

This is just the sort of crass arrogance we have come to expect from the FA, who have a distinctly patchy track record when it comes to attaining the kind of high operating standards we have the right to expect. Instead, they typically tend to dismiss attempts to hold them to account as 'troublemaking'. Of course, they are not alone in adopting this defensive 'don't be ridiculous' attitude to criticism.

The Italian football authorities felt the same way about their drugs testing programme in 1998 when the then coach of Lazio, Zednek Zeman, came out and said he believed the Italian game was rife with dope. Zeman knew a thing or two about dope, being from Czechoslovakia – a country whose history lay within the drug-fuelled sports regimes of those eastern European countries where the appliance of science in pursuit of victory was explicitly sanctioned by the communist regimes.

Zeman was slaughtered in the Italian press, dismissed by the footballing authorities as barking mad and pilloried by the fans for daring to cast such an aspersion on their heroes. But not everyone thought he was insane. A Turin-based magistrate decided to launch his own investigation. He discovered that Zeman was probably right.

The problem lay within the International Olympic Committee accredited laboratory that carried out and processed all the dope tests in Italy. The magistrate discovered that it had been common practice to dump tests results in the bin. He was also appalled at the lax system of testing. Firstly, there were not many tests taken in football at all and secondly, of those that were, there were instances of players and clubs being given prior notice.

The upshot of the investigation was that the laboratory was closed down. For the start of the season 2000–1 a new testing regime was established. So now, in addition to random tests at training grounds, two players from each side are tested at every Seria A and Seria B match. The findings of this new system paint a very different picture of Italian football. Zeman, it seems, had been telling the truth.

Paddy Agnew is the *Guardian* correspondent in Rome and he followed the story: 'We had players from the lower division testing positive for the steroid nandrolone and it came to light in a spectacular way when you had two of the biggest names in world soccer, Edgar Davids and Couto of Lazio, also testing positive.'

By the end of the season over a dozen players had given positive samples. So what does this tell us about soccer and the proclivities of professional players to take drugs to boost performance, or perhaps, more importantly, to recover from injuries? That the sport is rife with them? Possibly. That it is clean and the positives are the result of contaminated supplements, a fashionable defence among athletes of every ilk? Again possibly. That it only happens in Italy? Definitely not.

Concurrently there was a clutch of positive tests in Greece, the Netherlands, France, Germany and Spain. Greg Moon has a good perspective on drug use in a range of different sports:

> It does vary from sport to sport. Some you don't expect many problems and in others we are racing against the sportsmen concerned. Some are cooperative and some are not. The type of drugs will vary from sport to sport. But I find it difficult to accept that any sport, never mind a huge one like football, is completely free of drugs.

On the face of it, nandrolone (the substance that most of the positive tests identified) is a curious drug for a footballer to use. Athletes have traditionally turned to steroids to help them produce explosive bursts of power but this is not something that offers a special advantage in football.

However, they are also used to put bulk on to slight frames and, more importantly, they are used in general medicine to help people build up strength after illness or surgery. 'One of the aspects of steroids,' explains Moon, 'is they aid recovery from hard matches, so someone who has had a hard match on a Wednesday could take them to ensure a peak performance on Saturday or Sunday.'

Steroids would also help players to get going in the pre-season when most of the strength and conditioning work takes place. A lot of pre-season work is done abroad, where there is zero chance of being tested (the dope testers don't travel outside the UK) and if the drugs were used during this time they would no longer be detectable when the main fixtures start in August.

Sports medicine has grown on demand. The need to get expensive players back to the same condition or better than before is one of the challenges that has informed much of the progress in sports science in the past decade. Hand in hand with these developments, the profession's understanding of how drugs can help this process has also improved.

For Matt Yates the natural drug of choice for a footballer would be EPO (Erythopoietin), which is rife in endurance sports such as cycling:

> EPO would be great, especially for a midfield player. You would get 90 minutes out of them flying all over the place and then they would come out again and play a brilliant game three days later. With the right doctor you could have a programme with very few side effects as well.

EPO increases the number of red corpuscles (the agents that carry oxygen to the muscles) in the bloodstream, and

extra oxygen in the body improves a person's ability to per-
form endurance tasks. The other attraction of EPO for a
professional player is that it does not show up in the urine –
and a urine test is currently the only one that British footballers are subject to – so you would have to analyse a blood
sample to detect it. EPO is administered by injection, and
while Spanish and Italian footballers are used to vitamin
injections, there is no similar culture of using syringes in
the British game, which may explain why it does not
appear to have caught on.

But the times they are a-changing. A few years ago
only a handful of top flight clubs bothered to hire so
much as a full-time qualified physiotherapist but nowa-
days all of the Premier League clubs maintain a team of
medical experts. And an inevitable by-product of this
greater expertise and application of sports science to the
game is that it brings the dopers ever closer to their subjects. And as knowledge expands, so does the opportunity
to apply it, legitimately or otherwise. Until very recently it
was unheard of for club doctors to do blood tests on the
players in order to determine their pre-season fitness
levels. Not so now.

At the start of the 2002–3 season the number of
foreign players on the opening day of the Premier League
season equalled those of the home-grown variety for the
first time. So it is no longer true that the players in our top
flight are naturally antagonistic to scientific assistance.
Every dressing room has players from environments where
there is a more sophisticated approach to fitness and
performance.

Tony Banks is an orthopaedic surgeon in the north
west of England. He frequently operates on footballers and
has wide experience in the world of sport. His own sporting

pleasure is weightlifting, an activity where drugs are often thought of as endemic. He has also acted as a medical officer at a number of major international multi-sports events:

> The public attitude in track and field athletics 15 years ago was that there was no problem with drugs. That it was a peripheral problem, but of course athletes were taking drugs. We knew it then and we know it now. It would be very odd indeed if football, the world's biggest sport, could legitimately be singled out as a sport with no drugs problem.

Banks knows footballers use drugs. A club physiotherapist once approached him brandishing a bottle of injectable steroids that had been found in the dressing room.

> Clubs on the continent are usually attended to by a sports medicine practice on a contract basis. We do not have any such arrangement because sports medicine is not something you can qualify for within the NHS. There is no royal college to set the standards and train the specialists as there is for other areas within medicine, such as oncology, cardiology, orthopaedics and so on. The result is that our home-grown expertise in these matters is, by comparison, limited.

> Sports medicine practitioners in Italy, France Spain and elsewhere will not only deal with footballers but also cyclists, athletes and everyone else. Consequently, a doctor who works with cyclists, for instance, a sport widely believed to be at the cutting edge of performance drugs technology, will have the knowledge to apply, should he or she choose to do so, to athletes from other disciplines.

'You know what is going on with some of the big European teams,' says Yates, 'because I know people from athletics who visit these same doctors who are known for advising on performance enhancing drugs.'

It is doubtless still the case that most footballers would not think of using drugs to boost their performance on the pitch, but when it comes to recovering from injury you can see how a little chemical assistance suddenly becomes a very attractive option. Injury is particularly traumatic for a footballer, especially if you are a fringe player or under pressure for your place in a competitive team.

The point about football and drugs in Britain is that the expertise is available. There is the motive and the money to pay for the best dope doctors in the world and not much chance of getting caught. Like the rest of sport, football exists in its own global village. Footballers play and mix with colleagues from every continent on earth. Word gets around and the temptation, particularly if you do not believe you will caught, must be great.

No sport has managed to keep the dopers at bay. As long as the rewards for success are so great and players have the money to pay for the best chemical assistance and the masking agents that can cheat tests, then there will always be those who will use banned drugs.

The only defence is a robust testing system. The heart of any effective testing programme is random unannounced testing. Anything else is a waste of money. In the case of the FA and its testing programme, a waste of *our* money. And what is worse, it ensures that the structure for accessing and using drugs will grow and become more sophisticated. Every other athlete in the UK has to suffer the indignity of a knock on the door from the dope tester, so what is so special about footballers?

CHAPTER THREE

Take Your Seats

The Well-connected Stadium Seating Firm that Cashed in on Hillsborough

In February 2000 On The Line *charted the remarkable rise of a stadium-seating company that had been formed in the wake of the Hillsborough disaster and had dominated the post-Taylor Report demand for plastic seats. The company's prime movers were key figures in the game – former senior administrators and club chairmen. They had made millions of pounds.*

In the middle of a dour industrial area of Oldbury in the West Midlands lies Rood End Road. Most of the firms in this quarter of the Black Country are solid, time-honoured metal-bashing firms but halfway along the road lies a business called Pel, which, with its modern minimalist frontage and company logo beamed onto the reception area, sticks out like a sore thumb.

Interior design and project management are not the kind the businesses you'd expect to find in Oldbury. But then Pel PLC is no ordinary company. It is a group of companies specializing in furnishing and shopfitting and its key customers include major High Street names such as House of Fraser and Marks & Spencer. Yet it is doubtful whether the remarkable turnaround of this company in the 1990s, from a firm that was going bust in 1989, would have taken place at all if had not been for a sudden increase in the demand for plastic seats at football grounds. The men behind it are some of the biggest names in the game's administration.

In 1989 Pel (formerly known as Accles and Pollocks, a company that dates back to the 1930s) was losing money. It was a failing furniture manufacturer that specialized in educational seating – the sort of plastic chairs found in schools all over the country. In the summer of 1989 Pel was bought by Mike McGinnity, a retired Black Country businessman, who was a director of nearby West Bromwich Albion.

McGinnity had built up his own shopfitting business but, at the age of 49, had sold up and retired. Fed up with kicking around the house, he decided to come out of retirement after just five weeks. He told *On The Line* he was, 'talked into buying Pel' with the aim of setting up a specific stadium seating division. The company had flirtations with this particular market in the past – they had the tools to make the seats but the opportunities to supply them to the British sports industry had been few and far between.

Things were about to change. Pel would supply and fit millions of seats at football grounds. McGinnity, who would later become chairman of Coventry City, employed former FA secretary Ted Croker as Pel Stadium Seating's first chairman. Croker's son-in-law, Nick Harrison, was soon on board as sales director while McGinnity's former West Brom boardroom colleague, president of the Hawthorns club, and former FA chairman, Sir Bert Millichip (who sadly died in December 2002), would be employed as an adviser. Pel's connections would leave them sitting pretty as the UK's leading sports seating supplier. It would prove to be a very lucrative business.

The opportunity for Pel Stadium Seating to clean up arose from English football's darkest day. 15 April 1989 is a day remembered simply as Hillsborough – the day when 96 Liverpool fans lost their lives and hundreds more were injured in a terrace crush at an FA Cup semi-final between Liverpool and Nottingham Forest at Sheffield Wednesday's Hillsborough ground. The disaster symbolized the state of the national game. Although there were unique circumstances that led to the disaster, it could have happened anywhere. Decaying grounds, repressive regimes to combat hooliganism, scant regard for spectator safety. Hillsborough was a watershed. It was time for a change.

In the subsequent public inquiry – the infamous Taylor Report, published in January 1990 – Lord Justice Taylor called for 'the fullest reassessment of policy for the game'. He unleashed a searing attack on what he called 'poor leadership of the past'. The Football League and the FA, the game's governing body, he said 'had failed to give a lead on safety'.

'One would have hoped that the upper echelons would take a lead in securing reasonable safety and comfort for the spectator and in enforcing good behaviour by precept and example ...' said Taylor. 'Unfortunately these hopes have not generally been realized.'

On the subject of football club directors, Taylor delivered this damning indictment:

> In some instances it is legitimate to wonder whether the directors are genuinely interested in the welfare of their grassroots supporters. Boardroom struggles, the wheeler dealing in the buying and selling of shares sometimes suggest that those involved are more interested in the personal financial benefits or social status of being a director.

Taylor's interim report made no mention of all-seater stadia but after recommendations from the FA it formed a controversial part of his final report. In February 2000 *On The Line* revealed that some of those involved in football administration – those people so roundly criticized by Taylor – saw the massive stadium rebuilding programme as a commercial opportunity and a means of getting rich. The football directors and administrators of Pel Stadium Seating would make money from the changes implemented after Hillsborough

Graham Kelly, chief executive of the FA at the time of Hillsborough, recalled that he had rallied for the introduction of all-seater grounds as early as the evening of the disaster:

> I said we had to move the fans' preferences away from standing on the terraces and the view, generally, at the FA was that we should move to all-seater in the top divisions as quickly as possible. We took a view that radical change to the game was necessary because of the scale of the disaster at Hillsborough. It was so awful that we felt that in order to restore confidence in the game we had to make the bold move towards all-seater.

Although the all-seater recommendation was never made FA policy (they submitted joint evidence to the Taylor inquiry with the Football League, whose lower league members understandably did not support the FA's initial call for compulsory all-seater grounds), the FA's hierarchy did give evidence to the inquiry, recommending massive public investment in rebuilding the nation's football grounds. 'Six hundred million pounds was spent upgrading grounds in the next ten years,' said Kelly. 'It provided the opportunity for English football to launch a World Cup bid for 2006.'

The subsequent redevelopments after the final Taylor Report would provide a boom time for all kinds of stadium contractors, who were competing for their share of the market. Builders, architects, caterers – and the makers of plastic seats. Millions would be installed in soccer grounds over the next decade. Pel would supply and fit 60 per cent of them in the UK.

The timing of Mike McGinnity's purchase of Pel in the summer of 1989 came after Hillsborough but before the Taylor Report was published in January 1990. It could, of course, have been excellent commercial anticipation. But, equally, he was well connected. The FA's chairman at the time, Sir Bert Millichip, was a boardroom colleague at West Brom. Ted Croker, Pel Stadium Seating's first chairman, had recently retired as FA chief executive. This gave the company status and prestige. They would have access to the type of people who could give them work. In an interview for *On The Line* Mike McGinnity said: 'The seating market presented itself following on from Lord Justice Taylor's report. The capacity and the ability to make stadium seating was already there when I bought the company but the size of the market followed on from the report.'

Supplying and fitting stadium seats is not rocket science. An employee of one of Pel's rival companies, Metaliform, showed me how easy they are to fit. It takes seconds to drill holes into concrete and install the seat leg fixing. Then a seat ring slides on and you fit the back.

Pel were tooled up for manufacture before Mike McGinnity bought them. Making plastic seats wasn't the problem, selling them was. There was little demand for stadium seats prior to Hillsborough. Pel had dipped their toe in the limited market there had been – they supplied the seats for the main stand at local club, West Bromwich Albion, in the early 1980s for instance, but with clubs reluctant to upgrade their grounds until they were compelled to, Pel had installed just 4,000 stadium seats the year before Hillsborough. The year after, they fitted 40,000 – and it increased throughout the 1990s.

Back in 1990, for the handful of seating manufacturers, the Taylor Report seemed like an unfortunate blessing in disguise. Tony Sharrett, who was the managing director of seat manufacturers Hille, explained:

> Those of us in the industry thought that this might be an excellent opportunity. We'd spent many years in the wilderness with expensive tooling and facilities getting little business. There were a couple of bit players like Grandstand Tribune, who did some seating at West Ham, and SIS, who'd done some work in the north of England, but the major suppliers were Restall and Hille.

But it was McGinnity's new company, Pel Stadium Seating, who were to become market leaders. Sales director Nick Harrison told *On The Line* that by 1999 Pel had installed 1.6 million stadium seats in the UK and that their market share 'had fluctuated anywhere between 40 and 60 per cent of the marketplace over the last ten years'. Their millionth seat was put in at Aston Villa (a ground where Pel have supplied every single seat). Harrison, who joined Pel in January 1990, added: 'We tend to put in 150,000 to 200,000 seats a year. I think the timing with any business is the key thing and obviously the time for us in the expansion was right in the UK market.' He admits that Pel's senior figures helped enormously:

There is no doubt that the connections we have with the game, with the fact the chairman of the company, Mike McGinnity, is the vice-chairman (now chairman) of Coventry City. I think that has helped within the game. It gives people the confidence that we are going to do the job on time and on budget because the chairmen of other clubs up and down the country know they can speak to the chairman of our company very easily.

Harrison is Ted Croker's son-in-law. He told *On The Line*:

When Ted joined the company back in the late 80s obviously he'd just left as chief executive of the Football Association and so he was extremely well known, not only to football clubs but also to FIFA, UEFA and everything else. It certainly helped. Because he had never had any allegiance to any particular club he was seen as a fair-minded person so it was certainly very handy to have him as figurehead of the company.

McGinnity confirmed that connections were key to getting business:

We were very successful in Ted introducing us to the various clubs. What we set out was for Ted to endorse it. With his credibility it immediately got the confidence of the chairman or stadium manager. Although they had to put out the jobs for tender to three separate companies to satisfy the demands of the Football Trust who were financing so much of the rebuilding, it helped us enormously. Ted totally believed in the quality of the product.

In fact, Croker was wearing two hats. He was also a vice-president of the FA and it was in this capacity, rather than as a chairman of a seating supplier, that he was invited to address a sports stadium design conference in 1990. It was organized by Owen Luder, who was then president of the Royal Institute of British Architects:

> Ted Croker was one the top speakers that I managed to recruit for this seminar on stadia after Hillsborough, because clearly things were going to change. He started off with the words: 'The scene is set, the sun is out, the moment admired all over the world. The pageantry, the passion and the glamour of the English Cup Final' – and the background music was 'Abide With Me', which really was quite an emotional start to a seminar which, after all, stemmed from the fact that Hillsborough was a very emotional, heart-rending event.

For the chairman of a seating manufacturer this was an ideal opportunity to press the flesh and make a personal pitch to the people who could give you work. It raises just one of several important questions surrounding senior football figures who used their reputations and contacts for the benefit of Pel – in Croker's case representing the FA while serving as chairman of a stadium subcontractor at the same time. Luder remembers talking to Croker about this: 'He started off talking about the impact of Hillsborough and then, very nostalgically, ran through the way football developed and the way stadia had developed. He finished on this heartfelt plea that now was the time when we really had to get it right.'

McGinnity explained how Pel made best use of Croker as their chairman: 'Ted would be at a game involving a club who were going for a grant from the Football Trust to develop their ground. He would say he would be involved on some occasions. Would we be allowed to tender along with other manufacturers? It was word of mouth recommendations.'

Sheila Spiers of the Football Supporters' Association questions the ethics of Croker's dual role:

> You've got people who are directors of clubs and with links to the FA, and at the same time the FA making recommendations to Taylor about what should be in his report. Was there a conflict of interests with some people who suggested it in the FA report to Lord Justice Taylor?

According to Tony Sharrett, of rival seating company Hille, Pel made an immediate splash in the stadium seating market in another way. In order to compete they had to come in at a lower price than their competitors. 'They drove the price down and there's a limit to how far down you can go,' said Sharrett. ' Pel introduced themselves into the stadium market by advertising a stadium seat at £8–9. The average in those days had been £13–15, depending on the quality of the product.'

The first seating job that Pel undertook was the most significant and symbolic stretch of terracing in the Taylor Report – the Leppings Lane End at Hillsborough. *On The Line* discovered that after the seats had been fitted by Pel, the consultant engineers, Eastwood & Partners, had to call them back to make structural corrections to more than 2,000 seats.

Despite such a stuttering start to their new line of business, Pel rose inexorably. They would install more than 1.6 million seats in British football stadia – including 70 per cent of the seats in the Premiership. They became the most successful stadium seating company in Britain and their portfolio reads like a who's who of major football grounds: Old Trafford, Highbury, Anfield, Stamford Bridge, Villa Park, the Stadium of Light, the Hawthorns, St Andrews, Upton Park, Molineux and Highfield Road, the home of Coventry City, where Mike McGinnity is now chairman.

Pel have also installed seats at national stadia like Wembley, Hampden Park, the Millennium Stadium, No 1 Court at the All England Tennis Club at Wimbledon, Twickenham, Aintree and Silverstone. As Nick Harrison explained:

It expanded by word of mouth. These football clubs all talk to each other. One of the things chairmen will ask each other when they need a new development is, 'Do you know who does this, who does that, and who did your seating?' Someone would recommend Pel and say, 'Oh, you won't have any problems with them, they're market leaders and good guys, I'd recommend them.'

McGinnity said that carrying out work at some of the major football grounds in the country helped Pel's progress. 'When people ask you which grounds you've done and you start talking about Man Utd, Arsenal, Aston Villa, Chelsea, Wimbledon Tennis Club and the Millennium Stadium,' he said, 'it's not a bad recommendation to have on your visiting card.'

It is difficult to estimate how much Pel Stadium Seating have made because they don't file separate accounts from the rest of the Pel Group. But McGinnity's boardroom connections have undoubtedly helped.

In 1992 McGinnity suffered the ignominy of being the first West Brom director in the club's history to be voted off the board. He boasted to *On The Line* that Doug Ellis courted him for over a year and tried to lure him to Aston Villa. Ultimately, he ended up at Coventry City as deputy chairman in 1995, later taking over as chairman in 2002. All three clubs have their stadia totally fitted with Pel seats. There's nothing improper or illegal in that but McGinnity's association with them has given him the chance to talk business in boardrooms around the country. The sort of access Pel's rivals could only dream of.

On The Line asked McGinnity about his boardroom connections. Was he wary that some people might say there was a conflict of interest? Here he was, representing a football club at the same time as a stadium seating company. There are all kinds of negotiations going on between clubs, not least the transfer of players. Pel were supplying a key ancillary service. Was there a danger that to oil the wheels things might be confused? McGinnity replied:

> Not at all. We had the foresight to liase and connect with Ted Croker, followed by Sir Bert. The majority of football club chairmen and directors have been accused many times of the heart ruling the head but I can assure you that when it comes down to something tangible other than players there are many, many shrewd chairmen and football directors and managers and the only thing that would seal

the deal would be the product itself: the delivery time and the price.

McGinnity insisted it was the first time he had heard any suggestion of a potential conflict of interests involving any of the people associated with Pel, whether it was himself, the late Ted Croker (who died in 1992) or Sir Bert Millichip: 'If there was any possibility of any of the inferences down the line that you are putting to me, Sir Bert certainly would not want to be involved with Pel and certainly we would not want to be involved with Sir Bert.'

Of the estimated £600 million spent upgrading British football grounds since Taylor, £160 million came from public funding – in cash grants issued to clubs by the Football Trust. Awards were made by a panel of trustees from different sectors of the game, including FA chairman Sir Bert Millichip, who knew his former colleague, Ted Croker, was also with Pel. 'I knew Ted Croker was there, obviously,' said Sir Bert. 'I was a personal friend of Mr McGinnity. I remained a friend of Mr Croker during his lifetime and still remain a friend of his wife.' He also knew how successful Pel had been: 'I was aware they'd put in the seats at Aston Villa in particular. I don't think I was aware at that time how extensive their activities had been but yes, I knew they were there and they were there in a big way.'

As a trustee of the Football Trust, Sir Bert helped to decide which projects would receive public funds, and Pel were a sub-contractor in dozens of successful stadium improvement applications. Although he was not employed by Pel at the same time as being a trustee, Millichip, like all trustees, was supposed to declare any interests in bids involving companies owned by what are called 'known associates', a term that would include old friends or former colleagues. It is a system designed to ensure the integrity of this allocation of public money. Phillip French was a spokesman for the Football Trust (which has now been renamed the Football Foundation and has been given a fresh task, since September 2000, to revive the game's grass roots). At the time of *On The Line*'s report in 2000, he explained:

> Trustees would be expected to declare any interests they have in a football club, in which case they would be excluded from the discussions involving that particular club. They're very strict rules and they are adhered to. We have a list of declarations of interests and if there are doubts then trustees are expected to declare them. For example, Sir Tom Finney played an active part in the workings of the Football Trust, and if there were any bids involving Preston North End then Sir Tom would get up and leave the room or be asked to leave.

So the same would apply to Sir Bert and West Bromwich Albion, where he had been chairman and was a president. But should a trustee who had a long-standing friendship or association have declared an interest if he had been on the same football club board or served as chairman of the same firm of contractors? 'Certainly if a trustee was involved with a major contractor that was bidding for work at the Football Trust then he would be expected to declare that interest,' explained French.

'What about a subcontractor?' we asked. 'If the trustee knows that a subcontractor is bidding for that work or indeed that a major contractor has a special relationship with a subcontractor and is likely to be involved, then we would expect them to declare that interest,' said French.

In his time as FA chairman Sir Bert did not inform the Football Trust of his connections or friendships with people associated with Pel Stadium Seating. 'I can't see there was a conflict of interests anywhere along the line either with Mr Croker, Mr McGinnity or myself,' Millichip replied, when *On The Line* quizzed him on this matter.

After his retirement from the FA, Sir Bert joined Pel as a consultant in 1997. By this time Pel had exploited most of the seating opportunities available in Britain and were looking further afield. Nick Harrison told *On The Line*:

> We are now looking for expansion into the European market. They are, effectively, behind the UK market. The business that has been generated in the UK over the last ten years will move on to the European sector where they are far behind us. We've got to get our timing right in the European market and the new emerging markets in the former Iron Curtain countries. There are enormous markets there.

Pel thought a formal arrangement with Sir Bert, who was still an executive member of UEFA, would help, as Harrison confirmed:

> Sir Bert very kindly agreed to give us his assistance particularly in Europe – especially through his contacts at UEFA. He was a European consultant for about 12 to 18 months. He was a personal friend of Mike McGinnity's and was known to me from my

previous contacts and he was very helpful to us, but he is no longer associated with Pel.

Sir Bert insists he wasn't much of a salesman:

> What they wanted from me were introductions, mainly from clubs abroad, because they thought they were reaching saturation point within this country. I had colleagues out there who I tapped up to find out who was interested and who was not interested. I got some leads in the Czech Republic but as far as I'm aware nothing came of it.

Millichip confirmed that Pel paid him an annual sum, although he would not exactly reveal how much. 'Enough to keep me in Eccles cakes and gin and tonics,' was how he quaintly put it.

Although there was nothing illegal in Sir Bert's association with Pel, was he wise to work for them? During the making of *On The Line*'s investigation into Pel Stadium Seating, the english FA were preparing a bid to stage the 2006 World Cup. A sticking point had been Sir Bert's so-called 'gentleman's agreement', allegedly made with the German FA, that England would not launch a counter World Cup bid in exchange for Germany's prior support for England's bid to stage the 1996 European Championships. This was voted upon at successive UEFA meetings that Sir Bert attended. With Pel so keen to expand across Europe – and into Germany in particular, where the majority of grounds would require modernization for the World Cup – and Sir Bert's refusal to talk about his so-called 'gentleman's agreement' or his apparent acquiescence with Germany being the sole European bidder for 2006, his actions have coincided with the business interests of Pel Stadium Seating and could easily have been linked to his association with Mike McGinnity.

Pel sales director, Nick Harrison, readily admitted that the company wanted the 2006 World Cup to go to Germany: 'Obviously from a patriotic point of view we would like to see England get the 2006 World Cup, but from a business point of view we'd prefer Germany or some other European country to get it because they still have a huge amount of work to do.'

In November 1999 the British Council launched Football Nation – an exhibition touring the world to promote the best of British stadium design. It was aimed at building international support and confidence in England's ability to stage the 2006 World Cup. Geoff Hurst, Gary Lineker and Sir Bobby Charlton were among the many roving ambassadors who joined Football Nation's global trek. Despite their business preference for the 2006 Finals to go to Germany, Pel provided the seats for the auditorium and were the only seating company approached to advertise in the accompanying brochure. Alex Latimer, the sales director at seat manufacturers Metaliform, said:

> I wasn't asked and I can't honestly say why I wasn't asked. It was a British thing so all sorts of British manufacturers should have been asked to advertise. Obviously something which appears to carry unbiased recommendation is always useful. There was more than one contractor in the magazine and I would have thought they should have shown there is more than one seating supplier. It's a bit off frankly, particularly when you consider there are only three or four companies really making this

product. I think all four should have been given the chance so from that point of view it's a bit galling.

In 1999 the Pel Group was a £75 million a year turnover company majoring in shopfitting. Stadium seating represented a small, though significant (in terms of profile), percentage of their overall business. The post-Taylor boom sustained them through early 1990s recession and their dominance in the market owed an enormous amount to their connections. Legally, Pel and the people concerned have not broken any rules but their links with former FA figures raise a number of ethical questions – not least the morality of the very people so roundly criticized in the Taylor Report for having overseen the neglect of grounds that led to the disaster, then making money out of the stadium rebuilding programme it instigated.

I put these concerns to former FA chief executive Graham Kelly. How did he feel about his predecessor (Ted Croker) and the director of a (then) Premiership football club making money out of a disaster and, some might say – and Lord Justice Taylor certainly implied it – making money from the consequences of the mismanagement of the game? 'I don't have any comment to make about that,' said Kelly. 'I don't comment on people's personal matters.' Surely he must have a view? 'No,' was his blunt reply.

Sheila Spiers of the Football Supporters' Association wasn't so reticent. A Liverpudlian who was at Hillsborough on the day of the disaster, she thought those who remember the tragic events of 15 April 1989 would be disgusted:

The whole problem with Hillsborough seems to be it was the fans who suffered and died and they haven't got any benefits out of Hillsborough at all, and so many other people have. And this as an example of the people in the heart of the football organization and ruling bodies using Lord Justice Taylor's edict on all-seater to make large amounts of money is quite sickening.

Since our investigation the Pel Group has been completely restructured. It was taken into private ownership by Mike McGinnity's son, Nigel, in May 2001. Mike McGinnity, who is no longer a director of Pel, became chairman of financially troubled Coventry City in 2002, ousting his predecessor, Bryan Richardson, in acrimonious circumstances, which Richardson described as a 'boardroom coup'.

In the two years to the end of 2001 Pel's annual turnover dropped from £75 million to just £19 million. Its stadium seating market has decreased although it supplied the seats for Southampton's St Mary's stadium. Nick Harrison told *On The Line* that he was sure the company would offer a 'very competitive tender' to supply the seats for Coventry City's new stadium, which, when he took over as chairman, Mike McGinnity promised Sky Blue's fans would be ready by 2004. But with football's ever-tightening finances and Coventry being millions of pounds in debt, Pel may have to wait some time to tender for work at their former chairman's new ground.

CHAPTER FOUR

The Juggler

From Manchester United to Carlisle: The Weird World of Michael Knighton

Michael Knighton is the man who clinched the deal to buy Manchester United, then promised to take Carlisle United to the Premier League. He and Carlisle didn't quite make it – but they had some interesting times battling for Football League survival.

Michael Knighton first strode into football's consciousness at a packed Old Trafford on a sunny August afternoon before the first game of the 1989–90 season. Kitted out in a Manchester United sweatshirt and, for a near-40-something, somewhat minimalist white shorts, he juggled a ball on the pitch, dribbled it towards the Stretford end, then walloped a hat-trick into an empty goal. United fans, it should be remembered, roared back and he saluted them, arms aloft, beaming beneath his moustache. This was the man, the crowd was told, who had agreed to buy the club from the deeply unpopular Martin Edwards, and was promising to return the 'glory, glory' to Man United, who had not won the Football League Championship for 22 years.

Knighton unveiled his plans for United, arguably England's biggest club even then. He had agreed to buy the 50.6 per cent stake in United held by Edwards, whose father Louis, the previous chairman, had bought into the club steadily since the 1950s. Knighton, about whom the general public knew nothing, was paying £10 million for the stake and had agreed to invest a further £10 million to

complete the all-round cantilevering of Old Trafford promised by Louis Edwards' blueprint drafted in the mid-1960s.
'It was that which swung it,' Knighton said. 'Martin wanted
to see his father's vision fulfilled and I promised to do so.'

Before unravelling Michael Knighton's bizarre,
unique sojourn in professional football, which was to last
until he finally sold his 93 per cent of Carlisle United 13
years later, it is worth pausing to contemplate the deal he
had with Edwards. Nine years later, in 1998, Edwards was
negotiating the sale of United to BSkyB for £625 million –
30 times more than he agreed to accept from Knighton.
Edwards himself made over £100 million eventually, by
selling in slices the United stake the family had bought for
around £1 million. Knighton's near-purchase, complete
with surreal ball-juggling display, still sticks in the memory,
bathed in sunshine, as a measure of how much football
changed, so quickly, after the 1992 Premier League break-
away by First Division clubs and their subsequent multi-
million pound TV deals with BSkyB.

Knighton has since successfully sued the media who
repeated the story that he didn't have the finance to go
through with buying United. He had, he said, 'secured,
with the assistance of others, a £24 million overdraft with
the Bank of Scotland to buy Manchester United'. It was the
deal of the century.

Knighton told the press that he was a football fanatic,
who had seen through the stigma and shame which then
surrounded football – only three months after 95 people
had died at Hillsborough – and could foresee the commercial revolution ahead. He produced his own blueprint,
which talked about a stock market flotation and United as a
'brand' that could be grown and turned into a licence to
print money. As a major shareholder, he would make a

fortune too. This is now basic stuff but at the time the press ridiculed him: Football a business? United a brand?

The press delved into Knighton's background and the details of the deal, a spotlight that Knighton later described as 'tearing at his soul'. His backers, two wealthy business-men, Robert Thornton, formerly of Debenhams, and Stan-ley Cohen of Parker Pens, withdrew. Knighton, although he had a signed contract from Edwards, bowed to the tremen-dous pressure and pulled out. In return, he was made a United director and served a decent portion of shares. When the club floated two years later he was a director of Manchester United PLC. He has always claimed that his ideas kick-started the commercial growth that United has pursued successfully and remorselessly, ever since.

In 1992 he decided to have another try. He and his partner, Barry Chaytow, a Manchester businessman, scouted the country for a club to buy. Knighton, the foot-ball speculator, drew up five qualifying criteria, his 'funda-mental absolutes': The club had to be in a football town, have a large potential fan base, have 'brand monopoly' (no rival clubs too close), have 'brand potential' and have prop-erty around the football ground that could be developed. They looked at several but eventually Knighton decided that the lucky club was going to be Carlisle United.

Fans of Carlisle, England's northernmost profes-sional club, do like to think they have potential. Perched north of the Lake District, with no other clubs for miles around to compete for the fans' affections, the whole of Cumbria (at least) watches for the Blues' results. The club is most famous for their single season in the old First Divi-sion in 1974–5, which they briefly, exhilaratingly, topped before being immediately relegated. Around the Brunton Park ground were 130 acres, which could be commercially developed. But when Knighton arrived there the club was bumping glumly along at the bottom of the Fourth Division and, under the board of local businessmen, broke.

'In ten years' time,' Knighton promised, 'this club will be in the Premier League.' As at the other United, the club's future success and Knighton's were to be intertwined, as he explained with his natural gift for the soundbite: 'I said I would be a full-time tracksuit chief executive chairman. I would be fully hands on. The club couldn't afford to pay me in the short term, but I did say one day it will pay me a gargantuan salary.'

He told *On The Line* that he paid £75,000 for his shares, and he borrowed the money that would help transform the ground and power the club up the divisions. Colin Seel, a former Football League referee and lifelong Carlisle fan, remembers how seductive Knighton's vision was:

> He said, 'This is Brunton Park as it stands but wait till it is a stadium, 1999–2000 season, when we're playing in the home leg of the European Cup semi-final. Picture it: 40,000 people in an all-seater stadium.'
>
> I said, 'That's a wonderful, wonderful dream.' He said, 'It's not a dream, that will happen, you have Michael Knighton's personal assurance that that will happen.' I thought I was in the presence of a saviour.

Yet, still very little was known about this strange, articulate, booming football man who was embodying the new age of football as a business. Although he was usually described as a businessman or property developer, Knighton's background was in fact in education. In 1977 he had begun teaching PE and geography at St David's, a private school in Huddersfield for the children of the middle-ranking rich.

Knighton's energy – he describes himself as 'a total workaholic' – impressed the old lady who ran the school, Mrs Katy Wilson, and she promoted him to be headmaster in 1982, when he was only 31. He says he made money in the 1980s from property, buying and selling houses in the environment of low interest rates and steepling prices that characterized the mid-Thatcher years. When Mrs Wilson wanted to retire she handed the school to Knighton and his wife, Rosemary, on what he himself described as 'very generous terms'. By the time the property market crashed, Knighton says he had made enough money to move to the Isle of Man, become a tax exile and retire from teaching – although he held on to St David's.

The application of the Knighton principles to the underperforming Cumbrian football club began happily enough. In 1993 he appointed Mick Wadsworth as manager, a highly respected coach who nurtured an exceptional youth team crop, which included Rory Delap and Matt Jansen. In 1995 Carlisle were promoted as Third Division champions and also went to Wembley, where they lost in the final of the Auto-Windscreens Shield. Wadsworth left, to be replaced by Mervyn Day. Carlisle were relegated the following season but were consoled with another trip to Wembley, this time to win the Auto-Windscreens. The following year they yo-yoed back up. It was then, in 1997, that the Knighton blueprint, the rapid, inexorable march to become champions of Europe, began to falter.

Knighton had rolled his sleeves up and become a totemic figure to the fans, who had believed, had wanted to believe, in his vision. Still a workaholic, he was constantly at the club, having to be woken up some mornings by the cleaners, who found him asleep in the physio's room, as he remembers: 'For the first two years I slept many nights at that football club on rock hard tables in the medical room. I would turn in about 2 o'clock in the morning and get up at 7. When I look back now you could ask: was it all worth it?'

The project to transform the ground itself began with the construction of a new east stand, opposite the old main stand. While other lower division clubs were refurbishing or installing cheap, functional all-seater stands, there was to be no such modesty of ambition for Carlisle. The stand Knighton built, opened in early 1996, was huge, with 6,000 seats, incorporating 18 boxes, function rooms, and a space underneath, which he hoped would house the national football museum – a lottery-funded project that ultimately went to Preston North End's Deepdale stadium. The eventual intention was to create an all-seater stadium with similar new stands replacing the main stand and the two terraces, one of them open, behind each goal.

The new stand overran the pitch and Knighton's plan was to move the pitch and rebuild the stadium as part of the major redevelopment of the club's land. This, the 'Carlisle Gateway Millennium Project', including a hotel, golf course and lake for water sports and wildlife, received outline planning permission in 1996. The Department for the Environment, however, asked for a detailed environmental assessment, which was never produced, and in October 1998 Knighton withdrew the application. The east stand still runs 16–20 metres too long; fans sitting in the far end overlook not the pitch but the waterworks end terrace, which is now closed. The Football Trust provided a £1 million grant for the east stand but the borrowing by the club, guaranteed by Knighton himself, was to become the unshakeable reminder to Carlisle of their true place in football reality.

Albert Doweck, a Manchester businessman and football enthusiast who had lent £100,000 to Carlisle and become a director, believed the project was too grandiose: 'It was a very heavy commitment, in the region of nearly £2.75 million. I didn't think we needed such a big stand at that stage, we could have built it in two stages. It was a risk, really, which Michael decided he would underwrite personally.'

Some of the players signed at first to augment the Carlisle youngsters were also expensive, being paid fortunes for the lower divisions. The scale of borrowing on the new stand meant that by 1997 the spending began to slow down. Carlisle fans found that the European dream had reached its limits with a couple of brief stints in the Second Division and the Auto-Windscreens Shield. Mervyn Day left in 1997. It was said then that Knighton, always the frustrated footballer, became team manager himself but he has always denied it. 'I did some stretches on the training ground, but I never took a session and didn't pick the team,' he said. 'David Wilkes and John Halpin were directors of coaching. They were using me as a front man.'

Rothman's Football Yearbook, the most favoured directory, appears to compromise on this, naming Knighton as manager, along with Wilkes and Halpin as directors of coaching, from 1997–9. During this time, instead of the youngsters forming the core of an exciting new team, they were sold. In February 1998 Matt Jansen went to Crystal Palace for £1.5 million, Rory Delap went to Derby for £500,000, swelling a gloomy exodus, and in May Carlisle were relegated again.

Meanwhile, Knighton had made the national media again, this time for musing at a press conference about the time he had stopped on the M62 between Manchester and Huddersfield to watch an alien object flying overhead. Later, he made a cogent case for the rational possibility of the existence of UFOs but after his Old Trafford display, the sporting media were not generally interested in anything other than the idea that Knighton himself was on another planet. He fell out with the local newspaper, the *Carlisle News and Star* over this, and blamed their reporter for using the remarks – he said they were made off the record, which the paper denied. Relations descended into warfare when Knighton formed his own short-lived Sunday newspaper to compete with theirs, and peace would never reign again.

Relations with the majority of Carlisle supporters were fundamentally ruptured with the news that at least one of the promises Knighton made when he took over was coming to fruition. But it was the wrong one – the one about the club one day paying him 'a gargantuan salary'. The club's accounts revealed Knighton as a chief executive on between £100,000 and £120,000 a year every year from 1995. He also had his wife Rosemary, daughter Chevonne, and son Mark on the club payroll, doing various jobs. Knighton justified his own pay packet – 'It's what you pay, the going rate for a quality chief executive' – and said the other family members were putting in long hours at low pay for the club. But seeing Knighton make so much at a club which was by now shipping players and money was too much for many fans.

They also began to question where the money from selling players was going; it was the beginning of virulent rumour-mongering, which would from then on engulf Knighton's Carlisle. He acknowledged what was being said but has always denied the stories: 'Well of course people tell you I trousered the money. The money went on servicing the debt we had on building the east stand and other improvements at Brunton Park. It also went on land acquisitions which we thought were right at the time.'

In May 1999 Carlisle hosted one of the most extraordinary matches in football history. Needing to win to stay in the Football League, they were drawing 1–1 with Plymouth, when on-loan goalkeeper Jimmy Glass – signed after Knighton sold Tony Caig, the club's only keeper – went up for a corner and scored four minutes into injury time to keep Carlisle up. The story has a crazy romance, part Roy of the Rovers, part Billy the Fish – so fittingly Knightonesque. Jimmy Glass is still Carlisle's ultimate cult hero but what most newspapers did not print was the blackness of the atmosphere at Brunton Park that day and the fury that would have been vented on Knighton by many fans had Carlisle been dumped out of the League.

Reality had bitten. There was no prospect of change under the Knighton regime, which had run out of money, backers and decent players. Knighton by now could give an incisive lecture on the self-destructive economics and excessive player wages of lower division football, but being the practical experiment for such a lesson was no comfort to fans who had been promised a bit of Manchester United in Cumbria. The following seasons, in 1999 and 2000, Carlisle again finished 91st out of the 92 Football League clubs, avoiding the drop to the Conference in 2000 only by finishing with a minutely less awful goal difference than Chester City.

Then, in September 2000, with Carlisle fans now bitterly opposed to the chairman, owner and director whom they saw taking money out of a beat-up club, came dramatic news from Knighton's former life. At a court in Leeds, Knighton and his wife were disqualified from being directors of any company for five and a half and two years respectively, a serious sanction to impose, after one of their companies went bust. They had paid over £200,000 from it to their own holding company, Knighton Holdings, even though it owed the Inland Revenue nearly £300,000 in unpaid tax. The company in question was not Carlisle, but St David's, the private school in Huddersfield.

Michael and Rosemary Knighton did not contest the proceedings, brought by the Department of Trade and Industry, and an agreed statement of facts set out the brief, sorry history that made the couple 'unfit to be concerned in the management of a company'. It stated that from the late 1980s – the time Knighton said he made his fortune from property and was looking to buy the country's biggest football club – he had 'ceased to be involved in the educational operations of the school but remained responsible for financial management'. In that role he was evidently not a resounding success. Rosemary Knighton, it said, was the school principal and 'had little responsibility for day to day management'.

Knighton told *On The Line* that the recession of the early 1990s particularly affected the ability of Huddersfield's bourgeoisie to pay private school fees for their children. The court papers baldly note that the Inland Revenue were owed PAYE, National Insurance contributions and corporation tax totalling £297,854, going back to the tax year 1992–3. They had been seeking payment of arrears since at least December 1992.

From January 1993 to November 1996 Knighton had made 16 proposals to clear the tax arrears, offering payments by instalments and sending post-dated cheques. In October 1994 the Inland Revenue threatened to wind the company up but were persuaded not to by further promises of payment. The court document that set out the disqualification, a 'statement of facts not in dispute' signed by the DTI, and the Knightons' court papers stated that:

Of these proposals, four were rejected as being unsatisfactory ... in seven cases no payment was made by the company and in the remaining five cases the company failed to make more than one payment. Throughout the period from January 1993 until August 1995, the arrears to the Inland Revenue continued to rise.

The allegation, which the Knightons did not contest, was that the arrears to the taxman had run up to £288,463, although other creditors had been paid, and so the Knightons had 'caused St David's improperly to retain monies totalling £288,463 due and payable to the Inland Revenue'. Effectively, they agreed, they had used the taxman to provide working capital for the company.

In August 1995 the Knightons sold the school, which was the company's only business, clearing £369,278. At the time, 'in preference to the Inland Revenue [owed nearly £250,000 by then] and other creditors', they paid £203,379 to Knighton Holdings – the holding company through which Knighton owned 93 per cent of Carlisle United. Knighton Holdings had loaned St David's £365,312 and this debt was substantially reduced, while the taxman and others were left unpaid. On 23 May 1997 St David's finally went bust, owing nearly £500,000. Knighton Holdings' debt had been reduced to £161,933, while the Inland Revenue was owed £288,463.

The Knightons accepted that these two irregularities, the 'retention of Crown monies' and payments to Knighton Holdings in preference to the taxman and other creditors meant that ... the Court can be satisfied as to their unfitness to be concerned in the management of a company and that it would be appropriate to make orders against them'. Directors' disqualifications are legally enforceable orders and if they are breached, that is, if somebody acts as a director or 'directly or indirectly in the management of any company', it is a criminal offence, punishable by up to two years in prison.

In mitigation, Knighton had blamed the school's collapse on the recession; he asked the court to take into account his good character and said that there were no allegations of dishonesty against him. He also said he had personally lost £175,000 when St David's went bust. Shortly afterwards he said: 'All the funds from the holding company were used for the football club because that had become my principal interest.'

The court judgement meant that he had to resign from the club as a director, losing his £100,000-plus a year salary as a consequence. The deadline was December 2000. Almost immediately, his son Mark, a 23-year-old who had at one time been a trainee footballer at Carlisle, then worked on the programme, became a director of the club, and Knighton Holdings, in his place. Andrea Whittaker, an administrator at the club, became a director as well.

Albert Doweck took over as chairman and he tried for some time, together with other local directors, to buy the club from Knighton, but without success. Eventually, the old board resigned, leaving Mark Knighton and Whittaker as the only directors. The fact that Knighton still owned the club and had a son on the board of directors led to persistent rumours that he still had a hand in running the club. He and his son always vehemently denied this but the *Carlisle News and Star* obtained one of Mark Knighton's mobile phone bills that showed constant calls to his father – 58 in a week. Both denied that they talked club business: 'I do not talk about Carlisle United to Michael Knighton,' said Mark Knighton.

Local MP Eric Martlew, became increasingly drawn to the campaign by most of the fans and the local paper, that seemed to take over the culture of the whole city. In the summer of 2001 Martlew called for an investigation and he told *On The Line*:

> One of the allegations I have heard from a number of people is that Michael Knighton is still basically running the club. And as he'd been disqualified as a director, it seems he was going against the rules and the law of the land, and therefore I've asked the DTI to investigate that part of it.

On The Line was also handed a document, which purported to be board minutes, in which Andrea Whittaker seemed to suggest that Michael Knighton was still involved in Carlisle's financial affairs. But the document was false; Albert Doweck, chairman at the time, said the minutes were not genuine, and they were not signed. Knighton scoffed at the document, describing whoever wrote it as 'pretty sad and desperate people', and always rejected any suggestion that he was still involved in the club. Later he said there had been an investigation by the DTI that cleared him; certainly no proceedings were ever brought.

In January 2001 came another twist. Knighton finally announced – the news the fans had been pleading for – that he was to sell Carlisle. A quarter of the club was going to an individual, Stephen Brown, for £700,000, and 60 per cent had been sold to a company based in Gibraltar, Mamcarr, whose backers wanted to remain anonymous. Sceptical as ever, the Carlisle rumour mill was soon on to it. It took barely a moment for the city to speculate that Mamcarr was an anagram of the first letters of the Knighton family's first names: Michael and Mark, Chevonne, Rory (the younger son) and Rosemary. Knighton laughed at the suggestion that Mamcarr was really him, situated offshore: 'The anagrams you can put to Mamcarr are endless,' he said. 'All I will say is that this is a genuine vehicle and deal to transfer the ownership from Michael Knighton.'

Almost immediately, Stephen Brown went missing. The newspapers would later have it that he was 'exposed as a former curry house waiter with a beat-up Vauxhall' but neither of these actually qualifies as an offence or wellspring of personal shame. It did seem unlikely, though, that Brown had the cash to land him a quarter of Carlisle United, and he was never heard from in connection with buying Carlisle again.

The Mamcarr deal began to unravel. Knighton said he was waiting for 'clearance' from the Football League and the Inland Revenue. The League had simply asked who Mamcarr were, and received no reply. The Inland Revenue did have to be satisfied that the transfer of the shares to an offshore tax haven was a genuine commercial deal and not just a vehicle for avoiding tax. As it turned out, the deal never went through. He said the Stephen Brown affair and the League's request had scared Mamcarr away. Even as the deal died, he continued to say that Mamcarr had been genuine purchasers of Carlisle United, operating through Gibraltar, determined for their own reasons to remain anonymous.

On The Line interviewed Knighton in the summer of 2001 in Manchester. We had wrangled over the terms of the interview and eventually agreed he could be involved in the live radio discussion following the programme. He turned up in Manchester with a bumper-sized briefcase, his trademark smile, two or three stone heavier than we had seen him before. He doesn't drink, he told us, is still a workaholic and finds it hard to switch off. At times of stress, he said, he turns to food.

He had in his briefcase a pile of front and back pages, going back months, from the *Carlisle News and Star*. He said repeatedly that he had been victimized by the paper and was consulting his lawyers about suing them. 'Let me show you this one,' he said, then spent nearly an hour rifling through his papers, in his briefcase and plastic carrier bag, looking for a paper which he said was key to the whole thing.

When we finally began the interview, he talked through his time at Carlisle. He argued that his promise of success was realizable at first but over the decade the financial requirements of football clubs – most centrally players' wages – had mushroomed. He was, he maintained, genuinely trying to sell the club.

Speaking of his disqualification as a director, the events at St David's were, he said, a 'technical breach' of the law that he had decided not to defend.

Knighton was adamant that Mamcarr was a genuine deal. He waved a document triumphantly, saying, 'This is a share and purchase agreement.' He offered it to us and we had a quick look. It did indeed show that Knighton was going to transfer his Carlisle United shares to a company called Mamcarr, but inside, there appeared to be no payment for the sale. Instead, Knighton was to receive shares in Mamcarr. According to the document, therefore, Knighton was not finally passing on the club to somebody who might make a better job of running it but transferring it offshore to a company in which he would still have a substantial shareholding. Knighton said this was wrong, that after he took possession of the Gibraltar shares he would cash them in, selling for £3 million the club he had bought for

£75,000. 'What you've focused on, I'm afraid,' he said, 'and my lawyers did warn me, is a technical point.'

When we tried to probe this 'technical point' a little further, asking who Mamcarr were and whether there was anybody else involved but Knighton, he became agitated and turned the mini-disc recorder off. He would only say, when we had all recovered a mood approaching normality, that Mamcarr were 'some pretty high-powered people', whose 'desire for a degree of confidentiality was to avoid precisely the sort of debacle and embarrassing saga that Mr Brown caused'. Figure that one out.

Both Chris Green, the reporter, and I, had interviewed Knighton before, years back, mostly about his Manchester United episode. We got on well with him, and found him, as most people do at first, engaging, articulate, a visceral story-teller. After this strange interview, which took over three hours, we were left close to disturbed for him. His enormous weight, the briefcase with piles of old local newspapers, the pressure weighing on him – he had the aura of a man almost completely alone, yet still he declaimed with the same bombast justifications, the refusal to admit any fault. We felt a weird semi-detachment long after he had left, at 7pm, to drive all the way back to Carlisle.

The Football Association, acting on the persistent rumours, sent in its Financial Advisory Unit to examine Carlisle's books but, 14 months later closed the investigation. They confirmed, according to the club, that no charges were to be brought against the club, its directors or owner. In fact, they found a pristine set of accounts and legal documents, produced by prestigious firms. Doweck had always believed that Knighton was misguided in his ideas for Carlisle but never improper. 'Michael loved his lawyers and accountants,' he said.

This was a telling observation, we felt. Knighton's juggle on the Old Trafford pitch had announced to the nation – self-destructively as it turned out – an ego with an appetite. It went beyond the need for fame or acceptance by a game with which he longed to be associated. A PE teacher in the late 1970s, owner of a fee-paying school and property buyer and seller in the Thatcherite 1980s, the decade which formed him as an adult, Knighton's self-esteem appeared to rely above all else on his idea of himself as a businessman. There was the 'fundamental absolutes' jargon, his relish in dealing with lawyers, accountants, bankers. Even his fat salary, if you listened to what he said about it, was more about the 'rate for a quality chief executive' than a desire for the good things money can buy. Doweck, a man who loves his own pleasures, remarked on how little Knighton spent, never going on holiday or buying clothes or eating out. His weight, Knighton told us, was the result, mostly, of comfort-eating at the chippie.

The tragi-comedy of Knighton's tenure at the proud little Cumbrian club lasted barely weeks beyond the prom- ised decade. There was no sign of Real Madrid or Lazio at Brunton Park, but the inspired management in adversity of Irishman Roddy Collins in 2001–2 meant there was no need for a last game of the season escape. But after seem- ingly interminable negotiations to sell the club, first to a businessman, Brooks Mileson, then to Collins's Irish friend John Courtenay, things broke down in acrimony and Collins was sacked. There was time for another last roar of defiance, another strange episode, when Knighton con- tacted Mike Corry, chair of the Carlisle and Cumbria United Independent Supporters' Trust, and Labour peer Lord Clark, a lifelong Carlisle fan, threatening to take the club out of the Football League as a reaction to all the hostility.

The trust organized a boycott of season tickets for the 2002–3 season and in the House of Commons Eric Martlew raised the subject of Carlisle's mounting tax arrears. Courtenay and Collins fumed. Then, in May 2002, the Inland Revenue, owed over £400,000, finally issued a winding-up petition against Carlisle United. From there, it was a short jog to the end. The club went into administration – the chosen route of insolvency for the many football clubs going bust. Two months later, proposals were put to Carlisle's creditors and Courtenay bought Carlisle from Knighton.

It was an ignominious end for Michael Knighton's13 years in football, from his first sun-kissed dance in Manchester United kit to his exit, a banned director from a traumatized Third Division club sunk in administration. His time spanned an historically crucial period for the game, from Hillsborough – football's lowest ever point – through the optimism of ground rebuildings and new business thinking, to the clutter of insolvencies for lower division clubs in 2001–2. Knighton, a dreamer, an egotist, a painter of grand visions, was there throughout this time, on the wilder side of football, yet somehow embodying the core of its events.

A remarkable crowd of 10,000 gathered at Carlisle's first home match in 2002–3 to celebrate his going. Unbowed, he wished the club well. He always looked back at his deal with Martin Edwards and said that Edwards had plenty to thank him for: 'I'd have made an absolute fortune if I'd taken over Manchester United.' That is one of English football's more tantalizing what-might-have-beens: what would have happened to Manchester United, trophy-less for 22 years and in need of investment, had Michael Knighton taken them over with a £24 million overdraft in 1989? One for United and Carlisle fans to ponder, perhaps, over a pint.

CHAPTER FIVE

European Community

How the Legal Eagles Thwarted Europe's Biggest Club Collectors

Clubs with the same owner are playing in the same European competitions, threatening the whole integrity of the game and highlighting issues that will concern all football fans and possibly undermine the very reason they support their team.

It was more of a hesitation than a stumble, a momentary lapse in concentration perhaps, rather than a slip; either way, it let in one of the most prolific goal scorers in the League, and within a split second the ball was in the back of the net.

That slip, or hesitation, by Tottenham's talented defender Ledley King, allowed Andy Cole his chance and gave Blackburn Rovers the Worthington Cup. More importantly, though, it meant that they were now guaranteed a place in Europe. It could have been so different. If the predatory Cole hadn't latched on to the loose ball and hooked it past Neil Sullivan – it could have been Spurs waiting to be drawn out of the UEFA Cup hat to face Bulgaria's CSKA Sofia.

Lausanne, Switzerland, March 1999: some of the biggest hitters in European law are gathered before the Court of Arbitration for Sport. The case they are there for is 'AEK Athens of Greece and Slavia Prague of the Czech Republic v UEFA.' The evidence they were to hear and the judgement to follow was considered so important by

European football's governing body that they claimed the whole integrity of the game rested on it. For whatever the outcome of a match, the fans need to be 100 per cent certain that the result has been decided on the pitch and not in the boardroom before a ball has been kicked.

Although it was in the name of AEK Athens and Slavia Prague, the case was brought by their owners, Enic PLC, which also holds substantial or controlling interests in four other European clubs – Glasgow Rangers, Vicenza Calcio of Italy, FC Basle of Switzerland and their latest acquisition, Tottenham Hotspur.

The rule that Enic wanted to challenge in court was simple: clubs with a common ownership were not allowed to play in the same competition. But if they were to prosper then it was vital for Enic to have all of its clubs playing in the lucrative European club competitions. They were determined to get the rule overturned.

In August, after nearly six months' deliberation, the court returned its verdict, which was, in their opinion, that UEFA was within its rights, and the rule stood. Enic's whole ethos as Europe's biggest collector of football clubs was now in serious doubt.

Enic's story begins in the paradise setting of Lyford Cay in the Bahamas, where huge, sprawling mansions overlook the clear blue water, giving not-so-subtle clues as to the financial clout of the people who live there. The word 'Bahamas' means shallow waters, but it's been the deep pockets of one man that is behind the Enic dream.

Joe Lewis is a billionaire currency dealer and he bought Enic in 1996, slowly building it up. Journalist Dominic Prince has been following Lewis and his business dealings for some time:

It is a real rags to riches story. Having graduated from catering, Lewis bought a company called Hanover Grand, and they did outside catering. One of the things Hanover Grand had was a series of cashmere shops, including one in particular, based in Hanover Square in London. What Lewis realized was that lots of Japanese tourists were coming in and looking to buy his cashmere, and by the time they had to go out again to change their money they had changed their minds, so he started a bureau de change in the back of the cashmere shop, so he made more money from the back of the cashmere shop than he did on the actual cashmere.

Joe Lewis's name is a regular fixture in the top ten of the *Sunday Times*'s 'Rich List' but estimates of this secretive man's fortune are in fact just that: estimates. Even educated guesses can only hover at somewhere between £2 billion and £4 billion. His main business, according to Prince, is trading in foreign currency from his palatial Caribbean base:

At his house in Lyford Cay he has a dealing room that is like something from a Bond film. He has 20 people working for him, dealing currency, with machines spewing out bits of paper with reports from Wall Street, Tokyo and all over the place. It is very much an active business and he also acts with others for and against currencies. He has absolutely huge firepower.

Why Lewis decided that football should be his next venture is a mystery to Prince, who says that he didn't even know that Lewis knew anything about the game; but the circles he moves in may provide the necessary clues.

His friends include millionaire Irish racehorse owners and gamblers John Magnier (of the ultra-successful Coolmore racehorse stable and stud) and J.P. McManus, who have both built up a significant stake in Manchester United, and Dermot Desmond, who owns 20 per cent of Celtic. Neighbours on Lyford Cay are former Irish rugby international and now publisher Tony O'Reilly and actor Sean Connery, who, it is rumoured introduced Lewis to David Murray, the former chairman of Rangers – the first club to come under the Enic umbrella.

Football in the mid-1990s was the city's blue-eyed boy, but like many a high profile love affair, the city and football soon drifted apart, though never quite splitting up with bilious acrimony. Justin Urquhart-Stewart, an analyst with Barclays Stockbrokers, has watched the turbulent relationship closely. With the hive-like trading room floor busy behind him, he explained:

> The city get bored of new toys very quickly and last year's fashion tends to be this year's tank-top, so what you saw is people being rather dispirited by it – not so much that they didn't like football any more but they didn't exactly see the kind of returns that they had been expecting.

Prince thinks, therefore, that it was no surprise that Lewis wanted in:

> His real interest is making money. He sees that Rupert Murdoch is prepared to invest or buy Manchester United for £600 million and that it's worth

£1.2 billion. In fact he once got involved in a muted bid for Manchester United, along with Magnier, McManus, and another friend, Michael Tabor. He sees owning a football club, especially one like Rangers, as a commercial opportunity.

To those in the know, it certainly seemed a peculiar time to buy into football, and Enic's share price bore this out. For example, as Tottenham kicked off their 2002–3 season with a 2–2 draw at Everton, their share price stood at 32.5p, which was less than 10 per cent of its highest price.

Shortly after Lewis bought Enic in 1996, he appointed family friend Daniel Levy as managing director and put him in charge of the day-to-day running of the company. Levy was a city high flyer and a Spurs fan. On the first day of that season Enic's football portfolio looked like this:

Glasgow Rangers, Scotland – 20.2 per cent
Vicenza Calcio, Italy – 99.9 per cent
FC Basle, Switzerland – 11.8 per cent
AEK Athens, Greece – 42.8 per cent
Slavia Prague, Czech Republic – 96.7 per cent
Tottenham Hotspur, England – 29.9 per cent

In 2002–3 AEK Athens and FC Basle qualified for the lucrative group stages of the Champions League and Slavia Prague and Glasgow Rangers were contenders for the UEFA Cup. After the court ruling that clubs with the same owners couldn't participate in the same competition, Enic-owned clubs were once again doing just that.

In 1999 Enic wrote a letter to UEFA to try and persuade them to overturn the rule, saying: 'We feel that the proposed rule change banning teams with common ownership from competing in the same competition would be extremely damaging to Enic. Its implementation would be very harmful to Enic and it would materially impact on the clubs which we currently own.'

If the share price of the company is an accurate indicator they were, of course, correct.

On nearly every one of the 69 pages of the involved and sometime turgid ruling, the phrase 'integrity of the competition' crops up. One of the army of lawyers who sat before the three-man court of arbitration in Lausanne was Alisdair Bell, who represented UEFA. Sitting in his office opposite the Bank of England, he explained why they defended the rule so vigorously:

> There is a UEFA rule that would prevent two or more clubs controlled by the same entity participating in the same UEFA competition. And the reason why we have that rule is because we believe that there is an inherent conflict of interest, an unavoidable conflict of interest, if you would have two clubs controlled by the same person playing in the same competition.

If two clubs controlled by the same company face each other on the field, can fans be certain that the winners and losers are decided on the basis of what happens on the field within the 90 minutes and not in the boardroom on the basis of commercial considerations? An internal UEFA memo stated:

> How could UEFA guarantee sporting competition if two clubs of the Enic group met in the same competition? Who would win? Would Enic or its management decide or would the winners be

decided on the pitch, in a purely sporting encounter as desired by UEFA and its public? UEFA must take all legal measures possible to guarantee clean competition. The interests of clean competition in sport are at stake.

Bell helped argue this very point to the court:

We feared that there would be a public perception that clubs owned by the same person might not be playing to win, to put it bluntly, and that's a situation which we felt should be avoided in order to maintain the integrity of our competitions. I mean, there have been situations in the past; probably the best one known in the UK is that of Robert Maxwell, who tried to take control of Derby County and Oxford United. He was prevented from doing so and I would suggest that his subsequent business record strongly supports that it was a good idea to prevent him from owning these two clubs.

No one is suggesting that Enic or any other company buy football clubs to fix matches or to undermine the integrity of sport and no one could, of course, compare them to Robert Maxwell. Every fan watching, though, expects a fair contest to be played out – it's at the very core of the game. As Bell points out however, transparency is an absolute must.

Dr Bill Gerrard agrees. He is a lecturer at Leeds University Business School and an expert in football business:

If Enic had been successful it would have had grave concerns for UEFA. It would have allowed a corporation to build up sizeable indeed full ownership stakes in a number of clubs then compete in the same competition, and that could have very well brought into doubt the very legitimacy of that competition.

Dr Gerrard, a softly spoken and engaging Scot, played out one of the possible scenarios:

If you have got two teams owned by the same club, competing on the same basis, and if one of the teams has no way of getting through and the other does have a chance of getting through, there would always be the suspicion that the other team would throw it. That's why UEFA was concerned and battled hard to get that upheld. Certainly the court put a great deal of weight on the importance and legitimacy of contests, and the belief that these are true athletic competitions and that they are not being rigged through common ownership.

The court concurred, stressing that it was not so much a judgement against Enic but a judgement to maintain the legitimacy of contests. Its final ruling stated:

Due to the high social significance of football in Europe, it is not enough that competing athletes, coaches or managers are in fact honest: the public must perceive that they try their best to win, and in particular that clubs make management or coaching decisions based on the single objective of their club winning against other clubs.

Ultimately, the absolute aim of the court of arbitration decision was to eradicate any feeling that the fixing of matches could take place; in fact, one of its conclusions was that although there have been instances where matches have been fixed, it is rare, and when it has happened, the guilty have been brought to book. But, it continued:

> Even assuming that no multi-club owner, director or executive will ever try to directly fix the result of a match between their clubs or will ever break the law, the panel is of the opinion that the question of integrity must still be examined in the broader context of a whole football season and of a whole football competition.

The court found that the main problems lay across three issues, namely: 'The allocation of resources by the common owner among its clubs, the administration of the commonly owned clubs in view of a match between them, and the interest of the third club.'

In an attempt to match UEFA's firepower, Enic put together an impressive and powerful team of their own, including the architect of the Bosman Ruling, Belgian lawyer Jean-Louis Dupont, and top London QC Michael Beloff. They also enlisted the support of Glyn Ford, MEP for Southwest England and President of the European Parliament's Sports Intergroup. He argued that UEFA's fiercely defended regulation was contrary to EC competition rules on free movement of capital – the backbone of the Union. Sitting in the huge, impressive glass parliament buildings in Brussels, he asked:

> What is the rule put in place for? The rule is put in place, we would agree, so that we have a competition,

and so we can rely on both teams playing to win rather than one team lying down and dying because it's more convenient for the revenue stream or the TV rights.

As Ford recognizes, television is the important factor. The introduction of the Champions League was at the behest of the television companies, who didn't want the biggest clubs, and therefore the biggest audience pullers, being knocked out early in the competition. Hypothetically, if Spurs were to face Slavia Prague in the UEFA Cup, which of those teams progressing makes most financial sense in terms of potential audiences and advertising revenue to the owner they have in common? Not the biggest economic brain-teaser.

Ford feels strongly that the bureaucrats of Brussels were being over-zealous and that some sort self-regulation was far more appropriate:

> My advice was that they had to find a way of dealing with that by some kind of independent arbitration or some kind of self-imposed rules, so that the EC could say this was not necessary to protect the sporting side of what is a multi-million pounds business. The question is whether it is a proportionate response. The argument is not that the EC is going to say, 'You are not allowed to ensure sporting integrity on football,' they are saying, 'Is this the only way in which it can be done?' or 'Are there other ways that actually avoid you seeking permission to breach the competition rules of the EU.

Bell disagrees:

What the Enic case is about is really, whether sports bodies can take proportionate measures to protect the integrity of the competitions that they organize, and UEFA is pleased to see that the European Commission also seemed to have recognized that that is a legitimate thing to do and it doesn't contravene any provision of the EC treaty.

As it stands, the UEFA rule is clear enough, as it was when the deal to buy the controlling interest in Spurs from Alan Sugar was ratified by the Enic board in the spring of 2001.

Looking at the varying stakes of each of the six clubs that Enic has, it is difficult to argue that they do not have some sort of influence on them. What forward-looking company, having paid out millions of pounds basing its corporate policy on building up its football stable, would not want a say in how its course is steered?

From his University of Leeds office Dr Gerrard asked himself some similar questions:

There is concern, what exactly is Enic? What is its vision of itself five or ten or fifteen years from now? And what do the City see in a company that has located itself in the entertainment and leisure business with stakes in several businesses, which are football clubs. There is concern that outside Manchester United and one or two others, there has been very little sign of significant shareholder return from football.

Also, according to Dr Gerrard, the clubs they have chosen could hardly be classed as Europe's footballing elite; on the whole they are involved in small to medium clubs who require relatively small investment:

> There is no investment cost up front and those clubs
> run on a tight budget with the expectation that they
> can do reasonably well in domestic competition and
> have a run in European competition to generate a
> return on their investment. What they didn't want
> to do, and have never said they will get involved in,
> is a bidding game to acquire big stakes in big clubs.
> That would be very expensive and very difficult to
> generate any return on.

If these tactics are to bear any kind of fruit, then UEFA and
the European Commission will have to make a remarkable
U-turn, which they have not done as yet. According to MEP
Glyn Ford, it is down to how 'integrity' is defined, and Enic
need to persuade UEFA that their interpretation is wrong.
As it stands UEFA have the power to decide exactly how it is
defined so any change is therefore unlikely:

> Enic is going to have the right at some stage to chal-
> lenge this in the European court, and I guess that
> when it gets to the point where it is costing them
> serious sums of money they must be tempted. My
> advice would be to deal with the problem UEFA
> claim they have, which is, 'What is it that UEFA
> claims is sporting integrity?' Once that could be
> dealt with, then the rule will be one which is com-
> paratively easy to overturn. I would have thought
> that unless they come up with some way of dealing
> with this issue, then the Commission will call in
> UEFA's favour. However, if someone comes up with
> an alternative then UEFA is in trouble.

In June 2002, though, the EC's competitions commissioner, Mario Monti, did rule on the case after Enic appealed, coming down in favour of UEFA and their interpretation and upholding the decision of the Lausanne court. In announcing his decision, he reiterated its importance:

> The main purpose of the UEFA rule is to protect the integrity of the competition, in other words, to avoid situations where the owner of two or more clubs participating in the competition could be tempted to rig matches. Although the rule could theoretically be caught by Article 81 of the EU Treaty, it is intended to ensure that sporting competitions are fair and honest, which is in the interest of the public and football fans in particular.

But as the 2002–3 European campaigns began, only Tottenham and the relegated Italian club, Vicenza from the Enic stable, missed out. The full UEFA rules are there for everyone to see:

> *1. No club participating in a UEFA club competition may, either directly or indirectly:*
>   *a) hold or deal in the securities or shares of any other club, or*
>   *b) be a member of any other club, or*
>   *c) be involved in any capacity whatsoever in the management, administration and/or sporting performance of any other club, or*
>   *d) have any power whatsoever in the management, administration and/or sporting performance of any other club*

What is also clear is what should happen if two clubs with the same owners are to play in the same competition:

2. In the case of two or more clubs under common control, only one may participate in the same UEFA club competition. In this connection, an individual or legal entity has control of a club where he/she/it:

> *a) holds a majority of the shareholders' voting rights, or*

> *b) has the right to appoint or remove a majority of the members of the administrative, management or supervisory body, or*

> *c) is a shareholder and alone controls a majority of the shareholders' voting rights pursuant to an agreement entered into with other shareholders of the club in question.*

In the opening groups of the 2002 UEFA Champions League, FC Basle were drawn in the same group as Liverpool, while AEK Athens were placed in a different group with the Italian giants Internazionale. In the UEFA Cup, Rangers faced the Czech side Viktoria Zizkov and Slavia Prague took on Excelsior Mouscron of Belgium. UEFA's response to *On The Line* was to say:

> The ruling of the Court of Arbitration for Sport on 23 August 1999 was in favour of UEFA's stance and declared UEFA's rules prohibiting multiple ownership in European club competitions to be lawful. The modifications to the UEFA rulebook carried out following this decision and implemented according to the orders of the Court of Arbitration for Sport, and subsequently endorsed

by the European Commission, were in accordance with the Court's decision and reflected their view of a controlling stake. We have to be in line with the law in order to have workable rules.

This displays all the elements of a classic UEFA fudge. Just because Enic don't have a majority shareholding or a 'controlling stake' in their clubs, it doesn't mean they don't have any influence – it would be difficult to imagine a company as focused as Enic not wanting some sort of control for their large outlay.

As it turned out, UEFA were fortunately spared having to confront this, as Rangers were disappointingly knocked out in the first round on away goals by Viktoria Zizkov.

Enic's 29.9 per cent shareholding in Spurs isn't a random figure: if they owned just 0.1 per cent more they would be obliged by the City to bid for the remaining stock. They clearly do not have majority control of the club but there is no doubt that they are pulling the strings at White Hart Lane where Enic's managing director, Daniel Levy, is Spurs chairman.

The governing body has acted against Enic in the past; in 1998 they threw Athens out of the UEFA Cup because Prague were also in the competition. Alisdair Bell says that at the start of each competition UEFA asks the clubs to declare who controls them and to confirm whether or not they are in compliance with this rule:

At a certain moment at the beginning of the competitions we have to trust the clubs that they are in conformity with this rule. If it would transpire that there was an individual who was influencing the management or sporting performance of two clubs playing in the same UEFA competition, they would have to investigate that.

Every single club across the continent starts off the domestic season knowing that if they do well a European place is up for grabs, so UEFA must recognize that qualification for their competitions is an incentive. Bell accepts that this is a tantalizing carrot to dangle in front of the clubs:

> Oh absolutely, it is definitely there as an incentive and I can't necessarily deny that it would be for a club if it knew that performance in a domestic competition would not result in eligibility for UEFA competition, because a club owned by the same entity is already in a UEFA competition. It is inevitable that with a rule like this there are unfortunate situations that arise, but what is the more important objective to achieve? I think most people would agree that protecting the integrity of the game and protecting against conflict of interest situations is a kind of higher objective than the fortunes of one particular football team.

As Enic's interest in Spurs was announced, the chairman of AEK Athens publicly denounced the company for the way they have run the club. He told the Greek media:

> In this context, I am curious to see what difference Enic will make to Tottenham. Their investments in football clubs have failed, with the exception of Vicenza, thanks to an exceptionally clever manager, and all largely because of an inability or unwillingness to fund in accordance with their stakes.

His admiration for Vicenza couldn't have lasted too long, though – they were relegated to Serie B.

Christos Zeir belongs to the AEK fan club 'Original 21' in London. In the years leading up to Enic's investment he says, they celebrated three consecutive championships, but the success has dried up recently:

> We have the best team in Greece, I don't know how they got to such a bad situation, it's very dodgy. Enic have spent a lot of money but the chairman is changing every couple of months.

Christos knows that success for an English team will be more profitable to a company than success for a Greek or Czech team. It's clear to him where AEK stand as far as Enic are concerned:

> Maybe the lowest priority, maybe not a priority at all. I can recall two years ago when we were calling Enic in London to express our disappointment with the team. There wasn't someone to speak with us and once we sent a three-page letter expressing all our feelings on the way they manage the team. They did a couple of transfers and the next day it was in the Greek press that the fans from London were threatening Enic, but that wasn't the case at all.

Unfortunately, Enic is a PLC and such is the nature of that particular beast that it is the City who are answered to first, with supporters some way down the list. The company also has a duty to provide a profitable return for its investors, which is something that the court of arbitration had recognized in its final judgement. It is also conscious that priorities should be concentrated where there is more chance of a profit; this is common sense of course, but of no comfort to the smaller clubs. The court stated that it was:

> ... of the opinion that such differentiated allocation of resources among the commonly owned clubs is in itself perfectly legitimate from an economic point of view, and can even be regarded as a duty of the directors vis-à-vis the shareholders of the controlling corporation. In situations of common ownership the fans of either club would always be inclined to doubt whether any transfer of players or other management move is decided only in the interest of the club they support rather than the interest of the other club controlled by the same owner.

Enic are without doubt the biggest club collectors in Europe. The other high profile multi-club owner is French TV company Canal Plus who, at the start of the 2002–3 season, were looking to sell their stakes in Paris St Germain and the Swiss team Servette, no doubt influenced by the EC decision as well as their own massive debts and PSG's perennial inability to win the French championship.

In the vernacular of the competition they run, UEFA have that precious away goal and Enic's firepower has been snuffed out by a well-organized defence with the help of a sympathetic arbiter.

Multi-ownership is off limits, for the near future at least, but can Enic, having built their reputation on this philosophy, afford to back down and let UEFA have their way? Daniel Levy, bullishly, still believes they can sneak in a late equalizer.

You're never going to stop people that want to do dodgy things, particularly in football. You know some of the things that go on within the football market, and what UEFA should be doing is trying to really encourage transparency, and the only way you encourage transparency is to allow transparent public companies to be involved in the sector.

It's an optimistic view. UEFA not only have the European Commission on their side but, more importantly, the moral argument, and even with all the legal brains of Europe, Enic will find that difficult to overturn.

CHAPTER SIX

Boys from the Blacklist
The Innocent Fans Listed as Thugs on Police Databases

Fifteen years after the Heysel tragedy, the reputation of English fans in European competition still goes before them. Manchester United, Arsenal and Chelsea have all won trophies since the ban on English teams playing in Europe was lifted. But for the fans who follow their teams, the return to European competition has not been as successful.

The clubs riding on the success on the field have penalized supporters off it, incurring the wrath of the competition authorities and causing anger, misery and mistrust within the fans. They have denied supporters who have not bought all-inclusive packages the opportunity to travel and buy match tickets independently, and have done this with the full support of the FA.

Ole Gunnar Solksjaer's last-minute winner against Bayern Munich in Barcelona in the 1999 European Cup Final was the greatest moment in Manchester United's history. It was, though, the quarter-final victory over Inter Milan which proved to be the crucial game

According to Adam Brown of United's Independent Supporters' club, fans hoping to travel to Milan were told by the club that there would only be a limited number of tickets on sale for a stadium that held 80,000 people. It was well known, he claims, that around 10,000 United fans planned to make the trip to Italy. Adam Brown's experience on the night are in common with thousands of other British fans who follow their teams to the less glamorous and more obscure football outposts in search of European glory.

Brown tells of tickets sold on the black market for exorbitant prices; of being directed from the turnstile indicated on the ticket to a busier entrance where there was potentially a crush situation. Once they succeeded in getting into the stad-ium, they were subjected to a barrage of missiles from the Inter fans after being directed to a different section of the ground. The situation was then made worse, he says, by the actions of the Italian police who, having failed to act when there was a build-up of fans at the front of a queue, which they had helped to create, started ... 'Attacking and batoning fans at the front of the crush to get them over the barrier which they had no control and for which the fans were entirely innocent.'

In a report to the Football Supporters Association Adam Brown concludes that: 'Attitudes to travelling English fans must change and change drastically or this will not be the last event of this kind.'

He also gave this stark warning to the football authorities: 'Unless the Football Association listens to what its fans organizations are advising them, involve them fully in the planning for travelling to European matches and respond effectively to problems when they arise, they will continue to be partly culpable for events that happen on other shores.'

Since the reintroduction of the English teams, it has been Manchester United who has been England's most successful team. It won the European Cup Winners Cup in 1991 and had the famous triumph in Barcelona eight years later. The team has, though, faltered along the way. In 1993 it went to Istanbul to play Galatasaray in the Champions League and lost 2-1. Six United fans were detained in Turkey as trouble flared in and outside the ground.

That match proved to be turning point for travelling fans as clubs began to refuse to sell tickets to what are described as 'unofficial fans on unofficial trips'. The Football Supporters Association was less than impressed by this and asked the FA for clarification

The FA's Chief Executive at the time was Graham Kelly, who issued the following statement:

Having been made aware of various problems experienced by supporters of clubs playing in European competitions in season 93/94 the clubs had unanimously decided that tickets should be restricted to supporters travelling on official trips, which as you know is a practice we thoroughly endorse.

Adrian Titcombe, the FA's head of security, summed up the concerns about supporters abroad: 'The incident in Istanbul brought home the point we are trying to make, that it's not really the English hooligan that we're concerned about, it's the fact that innocent groups of English supporters can end up in the wrong place at the wrong time.'

In a statement, the Turkish authorities laid the blame for the incident in Istanbul firmly at the door of the unofficial travelling fans. Andy Thomas, a United follower, remembers though that the majority of incidents were due to heavy handedness by the local police.

'Very quickly people recognized that this was not hooliganism, it was foreign police victimizing a group of people. But after that statement the club still said this incident means that fans must travel with us. But the official trip coaches were stoned; people were hit with missiles; seats were taken by police, many people were not allowed inside, and those that were, were beaten on the way in. Very quickly there was an official line that was used and then taken back, but still that line was used to give clubs a monopoly on travel for whatever reason.'

The options for fans wanting to travel to watch their team are therefore limited: either they go with the official club trip or stay at home and follow the game on radio or television. The packages resemble long-distant hit squads – fans rushed into the town just before the game and then quickly whisked away afterwards, with no time to take in the sights and sounds of the place they are visiting or have a sociable and peaceful drink.

Andy Mitten, the editor of Manchester United's fanzine 'United we Stand', thinks that if fans are paying to support a club they should be allowed to have a say in what they do.

'If you're spending £300 to £400 you just don't want to fly in, watch the game and fly out. You want to sample the delights that a foreign city can offer.'

A government regulator, already well known to the football authorities, took up the fan's case. The Office of Fair Trading, which took on the Premier League over its television deal in 1999, stepped in on the basis that the policy of clubs selling tickets only to those who buy travel packages, was a restraint of trade. Adrian Titcombe and the Football Association were forced to think again.

'We certainly were suggesting that in the past, but it's been put to us that this may have been against the OFT regulations, so we no longer say that. However, we do support the clear consensus of clubs to control the movement of supporters.'

But in a letter to clubs, the FA continued to support the policy of linking tickets and travel.

This is concerned with tied-in sales, where one product's availability is dependent upon the customer buying another product as well. Expressed simply in football terms, it means you cannot have a seat at the game if you do not get a seat on the plane.

Not so long ago – in fact even more recently than their European Cup winning days under Brian Clough – Nottingham Forest's fans were planning trips to Europe's far-flung football outposts. At that time, according to Dave Pullen, the club's then-Commercial Manager, the club was making a loss on the trips it ran abroad.

'If we're talking about the clubs making vast sums of money from the tips abroad, then that is simply untrue. If we take into account the cost of the dummy-runs that have to be performed prior to the tie taking place to try and see that everything runs smoothly, I would suggest that we are not making a profit at all.'

It is the same story from other clubs. They treat the away-leg of a European tie as a loss-limitation exercise rather than a profit-making one, a strange anathema in today's ultra-commercial age.

When Alan Roberts was Leeds United's General Manager, he showed the sums to the Office of Fair Trading in order to illustrate the 'break-even policy'. He agrees with Dave Pullen at Forest: 'I've produced figures on this and, like most clubs, we have not made any money. The intention is not to make profit on the away-leg. Profit doesn't come into it. You make your money on the home-leg.'

Football found itself in a quandary because of the suggestion of monopoly abuse. What the OFT regards as a fair trading issue is seen by the Football Association as a threat to safety. Adrian Titcombe, the safety officer at Lancaster Gate, says his priority is the fans. 'We have to make sure there is minimal trouble associated with English clubs abroad and if there is any other legislation which impedes us from doing this then we have to be concerned.'

Titcombe then issued a warning to all English fans who loyally follow their team: 'We must face the facts that we are not starting with a blank sheet of paper. If there are incidents involving English fans abroad, the initial reaction will be to blame the English. If we have too many incidents, there is the possibility of another ban.'

The message from the FA is clear enough, but incidents like Galatasaray in 1993 obviously suited clubs and justified them keeping travel to European games 'in house', even though the evidence pointed to the English fans being innocent.

Adrian Titcombe says that the clubs have to be cautious: 'Clearly some people may argue that they are trying to take unfair advantage of the situation, but certainly all the discussions I have had, have centred on the very real danger of incidents jeopardizing English football abroad.'

The question of safety for the thousands of English fans who are simply intent on supporting their teams, came to the attention of Euro MP and football fan Glyn Ford. He was fully aware of how the current feelings on the Continent favoured English clubs as opposed to the fans. 'I know that you can travel to various parts of the European Community, four, five, six times cheaper than the costs that are being charged.

No wonder all this caused a fuss in the corridors of Britain's competition authorities.

The legacy, though, is felt most keenly by the supporters, denied the chance to follow their team abroad. The situation for some fans became so ridiculous that, in order to support their team, they had to make round trips of hundreds of miles.

Simon Mordue was studying in Germany when his team, Leeds United, was drawn against Stuttgart in the European Cup. He rang the club and told them of his situation: 'I explained that I was happy to tell them how I was going to travel, but their answer was quite simply no. If you want a ticket you have to fly back to Leeds, fly from Leeds to Stuttgart, then from Stuttgart to Leeds, and from Leeds to Germany.'

A dizzying and bizarre criss-cross journey across Europe for a fan who lived two miles from the ground. Simon told the club he would travel from his home and see the match independently, but he was told by Elland Road that there would be no tickets available.

'I sent off for tickets from Stuttgart and duly received three tickets in the post. I went down to Stuttgart the night before the match and there were hundreds and hundreds of Leeds fans who had bought tickets from Stuttgart.'

Fellow Leeds fan, Netherlands-based Guy Thornton, experienced similar problems: 'As far as trying to get official tickets, it's nigh on impossible unless you're willing to travel to Leeds and go on the Leeds trip – which, when you live in Amsterdam only an hour and a half from Eindhoven, involves a double trip costing £400 instead of £10.'

Leeds' response was to introduce extra pick-up points for all trips, but still it was not enough for Guy or his fellow european-based supporters.

Assistant Chief Constable Malcolm George of Greater Manchester Police looked after policing during Euro '96. He recognizes the anomalies in the way that clubs organize trips abroad, but says the first concern should be security. 'Security measures do seem to penalize the genuine fan, but any security means that a price has to be paid and the price is an element of restriction in movement.'

Such restrictive measures also mean that there will always be people trying to find a way round the restrictions. Thus, fans who have complied with the club and travelled the expensive way with the official tours have often, to their fury, found themselves queuing at turnstiles next to fans who have made their way there independently.

They do this through small, independent firms run from small offices who take fans to games around Europe much more cheaply than the clubs.

Leeds' fan, Andy Peterson, travelled to Eindhoven with an independent travel agency in what turned out to be an unforgettable trip. 'When we started examining the tickets they were all for different parts of the ground and we thought this could be a bit dodgy. Then two police officers came up to us and asked if we were English, if we were going to the game, had we got tickets, and where were our passports?'

According to Andy, when they said their passports were in their rooms, things then started to get a little nasty.'Immediately I had my arms thrust behind my back and they said you are under arrest. I was cuffed with a piece of plastic and we were taken to a number of coaches which were obviously waiting for a large number of supporters. We were told that because we hadn't been carrying our passports, which I believe breaks some ancient Dutch by-law, we could be arrested.'

The Leeds fans were herded on to the coaches. 'They had miniature Police cells on board them which were probably about three-foot square and five-foot high. It was the worst thing I have ever gone through in my life, and I paid to go through it!'

They were clearly seen as hooligans, intent on causing trouble and they say they had been warned that there was a risk of arrest by the Dutch police. In their opinion, the firms don't want to tell them all the facts and risk losing money.

One hundred and twenty three Leeds fans were deported, their personal belongings, including passports, left stranded in Amsterdam. Despite the authorities on both sides of the North Sea having their details, they were classed as 'unofficial' supporters and 'unofficial' in the Netherlands meant thug.

It did not end there for those fans once they got off the ferry back home. In the Netherlands, Lex Heiss had already entered their details on to his database at the Dutch Centre for Information Football Vandalism in Utrecht. He refused to say how many Leeds fans were on the list, but all those arrested with Andy Peterson in Eindhoven were on it.

'All people,' he explains, 'who are arrested by a football match in the Netherlands are registered in our database. So a local police force, which arrests a person at a football match, will send the person's identity to us and we will put it in our database.'

It is understood that The National Criminal Intelligence Service (NCIS) in Britain also keeps the names of fans detained abroad on file, regardless of the apparent innocence of the alleged perpetrator.

Gwylem Boore and his brother Rhys were experienced travellers with the Welsh national team. In 1990 they went to Luxembourg for a European Championship qualifier. The brothers were on a train, which was stopped by police on the border. They were hauled off the train, their baggage was searched, they were photographed and then allowed to carry on with their journey.

Two years later they were following Wales again, this time to Belgium when there was a voluntary identity check.

Gwylem and his brother chose to go through. 'I saw the police had a list and after I'd been let through the identity parade I walked around the back to look over the policeman's shoulder. I saw my name, my brother's name and a number of other people's names alongside the clubs they supported on the list. I was a bit concerned about this and my concern increased when my brother was taken to one side with somebody else and taken away to a Brussels police station.'

Gwylem claims that his brother was told he had been detained because his name was on a list of hooligans sent by authorities in England. Their mother, Anne, was given the same explanation when she made her own enquiries. 'If you listen to the duty officer at the British consulate, who was contacted by the Belgian police in response to a call from my eldest son, he was told that Rhys was detained because his name was on a list provided by the British police. If you read the documentation subsequently provided by the British consulate, they simply follow the later Belgian police line that Rhys had been drunk and disorderly. This could easily have been disproved if there ever was a trial because of the many witnesses willing to say what actually happened at the checkpoint.'

Letters sent to the Boores back up the name-on-the-list explanation and also confirm that the two men were placed on a police database after the train incident in 1990, when they were also supposed to have been involved in violent incidents. This, despite the fact that the violent incidents took part in a different part of the train.

All this leaves Rhys and Gwylem feeling, they say, very bitter.

'The idea of being innocent until proven guilty is reversed. You're guilty until you can prove you are innocent and even then that's not enough. We had to compile and amass a lot of evidence, send it off to various authorities, and say that what was being said was obviously not the truth, be it in regard to Luxembourg or Belgium. We have got witnesses, reliable people who can disprove the accusation which certain authorities have made and which has been accepted as fact.'

The Boores's case was taken on by Philip Leach, a legal officer with the civil rights group Liberty, who in turn contacted the European Commission. He demanded that the Boores's names should be taken off all lists. He feels the situation is totally unacceptable.

'The problem is that allegations are made and people, who do not have the opportunity to refute the allegations, are placed on lists. What should happen is that people should only be listed if there has been a criminal conviction. If this is not agreed, then people will not have the opportunity to have their say and will be treated as criminals.'

Philip Leach also handled the case of three Chelsea fans deported from Bruges. The implications, he says, are very serious.

'These actions by the authorities are serious and very fundamental breaches of people's human rights. To stop and search people, to photograph them and then to deport them involves violations of people's freedom of movement in Europe. The right to freedom of movement was established by the Treaty of Rome, and then supported more recently by the Maastricht Treaty. It is unlawful under European Union law for member states to deport people, unless there is a serious risk to public security – and that serious risk has to be caused by the individual concerned.'

The problem for the majority of peaceful fans is that they are tarred with the same brush as the minority who have blackened the name of English football for over twenty years.

Perry Ridley, another Chelsea fan, wanted to follow the club abroad and, after looking at the club package, chose to travel independently more cheaply and get his tickets from a Belgium friend.

'Myself and an Italian colleague travelled out there with ferry tickets etc., and there were about 200 Chelsea supporters on the ferry. We were all perfectly well behaved, but were met at the other end by the Belgian police. A policeman asked us why we were coming to Belgium. When we said for the football, he said I hope you've got a ticket. I said yes and showed it to him. By this time my Italian colleague had been allowed to go through. I showed him my ticket and he said it was forged. I said no way is that forged. He confronted me eye to eye and my mate said don't bother arguing – no one is going to get through. And everyone was turned away. All the police were looking at us as if we were scum. I was furious.'

So furious, in fact, he immediately wrote a letter to the Belgian ambassador to London. All he wants, he says, is an apology.

Two fans, same ticket, same destination, same purpose, but the British fan stopped while the Italian fan was allowed through. But that wasn't the worst of it. Perry Ridley had to deal with the possibility that his name was now on a list of potential football hooligans held across Europe and including the NCIS in Britain.

This apparent treatment of fans as second-class citizens was experienced by another Leeds fan, Stephen Davis, who travelled with a small, independent firm to

Monaco. His nightmare began at Dover where he met the coach.

'There was banging on the windows at every checkpoint, *zeig heils* neo-Nazi type chants all the way through. This went on all the way down to Monaco. The driver put a pornographic film on the video. As soon as it was put on, a man said, look, you can't have this on I have a nine-year-old kid. The driver turned it off, but, after that, the bloke got abuse all the way through and was threatened at a service station as well.'

The small firms are quick to defend their tours and have banned the hooligan element concerned. They stress that they do all they can to keep the hooligans from travelling abroad.

The confusion that results from fans using 'official' and 'unofficial' tours means that segregation – a vital method of crowd-control – goes out of the window. Alan Roberts was the General Manger of Leeds United during the European Cup campaign. He says he understands fans wanting to see the team, but selling tickets to fans in the home-end is asking for trouble.

'What I can't condone is anybody knowingly selling tickets in the wrong area. All our fans know that a segregation policy exists; and that buying a ticket for the wrong end means risking not getting in and wasting their money.'

UEFA rules dictate that away-fans should be segregated, but the small firms have a simple way of getting hold of tickets, the just go directly to the European clubs to buy them – only though, after they have approached the clubs at home who almost inevitably turn their request down.

They say that there are still safeguards in place by the home club, and deny that they are behaving irresponsibly. Indeed, they make the assertion that some fans would not get to see the games without the existence of such firms and that others would still travel to matches, but with even less control. Rather than being attacked, they feel in fact that they should be commended for the service they provide.

Glyn Ford and his Brussels colleagues have answers to the problem of segregation and to mistaking football fans for football hooligans. 'Rather than indicting a whole category of people, and making them second-class citizens, the solution seems to be that we should identify the perpetrators, give them the criminal records they deserve, and then stop them travelling on the basis of their records.'

Punish the thugs and give freedom to the fans. Simple, in theory. But the hooligan will always slip through the net. Malcolm George of Greater Manchester Police is convinced that the genuine fan needs more protection. 'It offends me that people can go to a game with no intention of being part of the game in the usual sense. They go to commit criminal acts of violence, and to manipulate situations so that they aren't actually putting the boot in, and can clear off as the trouble starts. Those people steer free of justice and that offends me as much as it does the genuine fan.'

A hooligan database like that of Lex Heiss in Holland is a dangerous method to combat hooliganism in Europe. In some respects, the English fan should be prepared to face the consequences in countries which have suffered, time after time, at the hands of followers at club and international level. But this means that the majority of innocent fans will have to go on paying for the sins of the few.

The clubs and FA, sick of having their names dragged through the mud, and mindful that another Heysel or Galatasaray may be around the corner, decided that some controls were needed. But these, in turn, caused more problems. Euro hit-lists, over-zealous policing and ticket policies falling foul of the competition authorities, all came about as direct consequences of the hooligans' reign of terror.

The solution, Glyn Ford feels, is not to restrict all football fans *en masse*, but 'to identify which football fans are uncontrollable hooligans'. One can't imagine another category of people, who are seen differently on different days of the week. Identify the people, convict them, then restrict their movement rather than everybody else's.'

Incidents at the World Cup show that the age of the organized hooligan is not dead, and that the onus is now on clubs and countries to make sure that fans like Gwylem and Rhys Boore are not penalized for life.

CHAPTER SEVEN

The Friendly Club

Cosy Deals and Abuse of Trust at Stockport County

You would love to love the lower division club battling for attention in the shadow of its giant Manchester neighbours. But Stockport County's rise to the First Division was accompanied by inflated invoices, struck-off companies applying for grant-aided work on the ground, and an industrial tribunal's damning judgment of its treatment of the club's most celebrated manager.

Stockport County is English football's self-styled 'friendly club', a sobriquet which smiles on the public face of a club battling doughtily for its identity, much like Stockport itself, which resists being absorbed by the sprawl of Manchester, ten miles to the north. For much of the club's 120-year history there was not too much for County's fans to celebrate, other than being friendly and local; the club scudded around the bottom of the Football League, giving the odd ex-Manchester City or United playing legend a final pay packet on their way down and out of football.

This small town inferiority complex began to change after 1988, when the local professionals and businessmen who made up the club board stood aside for a new major shareholder and chairman. His name was Brendan Elwood, a landlord from Sheffield, who had been looking for some time to invest in football. For all the rancour and bitterness that would ultimately blacken Elwood's time at County, his chairmanship produced the club's most successful ever spell on the field, achieved through his initially inspired recruitment of managers.

Elwood's first appointment to the manager's battered office in County's rundown Edgeley Park ground, in 1989, would furnish future pub quiz compilers with a nice teaser: who was the first foreigner to manage a club in English football, the first to work with an England team? Not Arsène Wenger, the future pub quiz teams should conclude. Nor Ruud Gullit, nor Sven-Goran Eriksson. In fact, it was a little Uruguayan, who had clambered indefatigably through the jungle of English football since, speaking little English, he hustled his first coaching job at Luton Town when he arrived in Britain in the 1970s. His methods, rooted in obsessive work on players' individual technique, had been recognized on coaching courses by the Football Association and in 1980-2 he was asked to work as a coach with England youth sides. He has the squad picture in the scrapbook of an extraordinary career, featuring him, the first foreigner to line up for an England team picture, standing proudly with three lions on his tracksuit chest – Danny Bergara.

An enthusiast, a life force, Bergara moved to Sheffield United but lost his job in favour of bigger names, appointed by chairmen to curry favour and headlines, if not enduring success. He settled in the area but was out of work and coaching Sheffield, the famous amateur club, believed to be the world's oldest, when Elwood saw him at work and spotted his winning way with players.

Bergara managed to land his first manager's job in 1988, at Rochdale, another club not lounging in the glamour end of the North west's family of professional clubs. He tells a laugh-out-loud story about mice in his Spotland office eating into his kit bag and munching the chocolate bar he had salted away for a long away trip. The following year, Elwood, by now Stockport's chairman, offered him the manager's job there and he accepted. 'It was my chance,' he said. 'I'd worked so hard for it, and I was determined to be successful.'

The plan to turn Stockport around began with what might be termed the infrastructure, as Bergara remembers:

> The dressing rooms were disgusting, filthy, there were nails sticking out. I said I wanted them repaired, painted. The players had too little respect for the club and themselves; they were walking around the showers barefoot and I insisted they wore flip-flops to stop them slipping.

He introduced changes to the playing methods, training practices, and tactics. Briskly, defiantly, he insisted that Stockport was not a suburban dumping ground in the shadow of its Manchester giant neighbours but a club with its own history, dignity and a few thousand loyal supporters who deserved self-respect too.

Two years later, having occupied the Fourth Division for 21 years, Stockport won promotion. The following years, 1992 and 1993, they went to Wembley for the final of the Autoglass Trophy, although, as with two Wembley appearances in play-off finals, they trudged back up the M6 as losers. Bergara became a hero, loved by the fans for his enthusiasm and his passion for the game, communicated in a unique Manc-Uruguayan accent. He showed a talent for finding players who were underachieving elsewhere, coaching them into unprecedented form and, given Stockport's place in football's food chain, selling them at a profit to bigger clubs.

Kevin Francis, the 6 foot 7 inch centre forward signed from Derby, also became a cult figure for the fans, pulling apart lower division defences, who couldn't cope with his size. He scored freely for Stockport before the club sold him to Birmingham City for £800,000. Bergara wrought exceptional performances from other players, such as Andy Preece, Alun Armstrong and Paul Williams, who had never previously excelled, earning handsome transfer fees for Elwood's Stockport from bigger clubs. It was a measure of his coaching skills that many of the players never really achieved much when they left him.

For the first time money came to Stockport County, and as a coach Bergara felt that not enough was spent to improve a bumpy, rutted pitch. The money was spent on the ground. Elwood set about rebuilding Edgeley Park, a job required following the 1989 Hillsborough disaster and subsequent Taylor Report, which called for wholesale improvements to Britain's crumbling football grounds.

A man who would be key to the rebuilding of Edgeley Park was another director, Mike Baker. He is a builder, whose company, Ellenby Construction, a small firm based in Bolton, was to carry out almost all the work on the ground. As recently as 1991 Ellenby recorded an annual profit of only £990 but the work awarded to him at Stockport was to make Baker's name as a builder of football grounds – and his and his company's fortune. *On The Line* went to see him in his bright new two-storey office block in Bolton, which is decorated inside with pictures of the new stands Ellenby have built at Stockport and at several clubs since, including Mansfield Town, Bradford City, Rochdale and a handful of others across the North.

Baker told us that his route to the Edgeley Park board-room was not quite the usual one of supporter-made-good sending a few quid the way of his beloved club. Ellenby had in 1987 carried out some routine work on the railway end terrace at Edgeley Park and the struggling, pre-Elwood club hadn't been able to pay for it. Baker had threatened to put them out of existence. 'At one time I was in possession of a winding-up order against the club,' he said. As a device to fend off liquidation, the club suggested he become a director: 'I was approached by the then chairman, Josh Lewis, to see if I would be prepared to join the board almost as an overseeing role until the club were able to pay us.'

Baker said that after going along to Edgeley Park for a few matches he became a fan: 'I was hooked and have been hooked on Stockport County ever since.'

It was to prove a happy addiction for Baker and his small building firm. The improvements to football grounds insisted upon by the government after the Taylor Report were helped by some £200 million in public money, made available in grants by the Football Trust. Many people believe in retrospect that too little was asked of the clubs in return for these grants. Some now argue that the money should have been paid in the form of low interest loans, which could have been repaid by the clubs when they landed in richer times. As early as 1992 football had its commercial bonanza, with Sky TV paying millions to the Premier League, yet the clubs, even the richest in the country, who would soon make millions floating on the stock exchange, were still given grants to build the new stands.

The Football Trust counter any such reservations by pointing out that their prime concern was to improve safety following the horrific loss of life at Hillsborough, and that the timescale for improving ragged grounds at most of the 92 professional clubs was too urgent for too many bureaucratic safeguards. The system was nevertheless intended to be reasonably tight, to procure the rebuilding at reasonable prices and thereby ensure that the public money was responsibly spent.

The clubs had to show on their grant applications to the Trust that the work was necessary to improve their grounds or that it would allow them to comply with post-Taylor Report regulations. They also had to provide three 'properly authenticated competitive tenders' for any job and the Trust's rules required them to disclose any connections between a director of a club and a building contractor; the Trust would take such associations into account when assessing the tenders. As long as the Trust considered that the tenders were genuinely competitive, they awarded the grants according to the lowest quoted price. This basic system was intended to allow the grounds to be rebuilt quickly while protecting the club and the public money administered by the trust. The point of the tendering process was to ensure that pricing was competitive and that there was no question of fixing a price that would increase the amount of public money spent.

At Stockport more than £2 million, much of it subsidized with grants from the Trust, was spent converting Edgeley Park from a crumbling old Fourth Division ground to post-Taylor Report respectability. The bulk of the money was paid to Mike Baker's company, which was awarded all the serious work. The key project for him was the rebuilding of the all-seater Cheadle end, the home fans' favoured position behind the goal. Baker, speaking of his company, described it as 'our breakthrough' – the major stand that helped Ellenby win other work at northern football grounds. For that job, Baker's company did indeed come in cheapest in a competitive tender with two large building companies.

But *On The Line* learned that for two of the jobs, one for re-seating Stockport's main stand, the other for extending a car park, Baker's company won the work with tenders that were pitched against two other companies well-known to him. On neither occasion, we were led to understand, were either of the connections disclosed to the Football Trust. Of the other two firms whom Stockport invited to tender against Baker, one was based in Bolton. Baker knew one of their senior staff: 'They have a director who once worked for me,' he admitted. Both he and the company denied they discussed the contract before tendering.

Behind the other company, which was called Field Acre Construction, lay a more intriguing tale. Baker told us, quite openly, when we interviewed him, that the owner of Field Acre, who put the tender in, Tony Marland, was known to him. 'I was at college with Tony Marland,' he said. 'We went on the same course.'

Not only that, but Baker actually called Marland to tell him he had suggested Field Acre to the club's architects. He even gave Marland a rough figure, 'less than £100,000 or something of that order', and then personally enquired if he would bid – for a job against Baker's own company. 'I think I told Tony, "I've put your name forward",' he said. "Do you want to price a job of this order?"'

The Football Trust received tenders for both jobs, in 1995 and 1996, from Ellenby, the Bolton company and Field Acre. For the re-seating job, the Bolton company's tender was for £89,000 and Field Acre's was for £86,000. Ellenby came in at £79,000 and so, according to Trust rules, the Stockport County director was awarded another piece of work at Edgeley Park, for which his company was paid.

The most curious point of all was really quite fundamental. Marland's company, Field Acre, which had been so narrowly thwarted in its attempt to win this work, did not in fact exist. It had packed up, ceased trading. It had even been struck off the company register in 1987 – eight years before bidding for the work. So when Baker invited his old college mate to tender against him for the re-seating contract, Marland did so on behalf of a company that he knew had been dissolved some years before.

Baker and Marland both deny there was anything untoward in this. Marland said that the company was trying to get back into business in the mid-1990s and had gone after a few contracts then. Baker said that he had not known Marland had ceased trading eight years earlier: 'I had not spoken to him for some time. When I rang him to say that I had put his name forward to the club's architects, he told me that Field Acre had not been trading but he was looking to restart Field Acre.'

The Football Trust, administering public money to repair grounds after 96 Liverpool supporters were killed in the terrible crush at Hillsborough, asked for three 'properly authenticated competitive tenders', and for connections between directors and contractors to be disclosed. The clubs, private companies, had only to comply with these basic requirements to have cheques written out to them. It was an almost uniquely generous system, set up after football's own neglect had produced such tragedy. At Stockport, the company of one of the directors was paid for work after bids were received against his – one from a company with a director who used to work for him, the other from an old college mate, in the name of a company struck off the register eight years before.

On The Line put it to Baker that what had happened could sound like collusion – precisely what the Trust's rules were designed to prevent. 'Well, I hope it does not,' he said, 'because there has been no collusion. We are submitting our prices in a bona fide way and they are there to be beaten or not ... I am not going to apologize for being successful.'

In another case involving work at Stockport, *On The Line* found a flagrant breach of the Trust's rules and procedures. The Trust had agreed to pay 75 per cent of the cost of installing a new PA system, an important safety feature. A local firm, Delta Communications, sitting on the A6 three miles from Edgeley Park, were, to the delight of its proprietor, Alan Ratcliffe, invited by the club to tender for the job. The price, confirmed by Ratcliffe to us, was £41,750. This included, he also confirmed to us, very clearly, the cost of the work and, in a competitive market, Delta's profit. It was by far the lowest bid submitted and so Delta were given the job.

Then Ratcliffe was invited down to Edgeley Park to discuss the detail with Stockport's then chief executive, David Coxon. Ratcliffe told us that Coxon suggested that Delta should increase their invoice, but the extra money, it was made clear, would be paid back to the club, not go to Delta.

Ratcliffe said Coxon asked him to lay the figures out in a memo, which he did. *On The Line* obtained a copy of it. It showed that the price eventually put in was £59,999, a penny short of £60,000, nearly £20,000 more than the true price of the job. The application Stockport sent in to the Football Trust stated the higher price, £59,999. This was still the lowest tender and the Trust duly paid Stockport County 75 per cent of it: £44,999. The grant awarded, therefore, was £3,000 more than the real cost of the job. Stockport paid Delta the full £59,999 but Ratcliffe was immediately required to pay back the difference of just over £18,000. This, the club said, was for 'sponsorship'. Ratcliffe confirmed that the club gave Delta hoardings round the ground for two years, scoreboard advertising, a lounge facility and 'various other small items over a period of time'. He admitted that the invoice for the work was inflated beyond its true value – which included his profit – but said he did not know where the club was getting the money from and certainly had no idea that they were going to apply to the Football Trust for a grant, or that their application for the money had been successful.

David Coxon told us *On The Line* that he could not remember the incident and that all his files were at the club, so suggested we contact the club secretary, Gary Glendinning, who issued the following statement: 'Three independent tenders were submitted of which Delta Telecom were the cheapest at £59,999; this amount was paid in full. Delta Telecom subsequently re-invested their profit on the project by way of a two-year sponsorship agreement worth £18,315, which was their perogative.'

But Ratcliffe insists that this was simply not the case, that the original price of £41,750 included his profit, 'a low profit margin', and that his invoice was inflated at the suggestion of Coxon, the then chief executive of the club. *On The Line* asked him, 'The actual price of the job was £41,750, is that right?', and he replied:

> It was at that particular time, yes. I was concerned about the increase in price, about the way it was put to me. It was an increase in profit although that profit never came to us. I do remember a conversation with Mr Coxon. It was suggested to me that our profit was very low in the first place, there might be room for manoeuvre and because of that, yes, we did inflate our profit if you like, which was turned back to sponsorship.

We asked Ratcliffe to confirm how this worked, that when Coxon had said 'room for manoeuvre', he meant that the price for the job could be inflated.

> 'Yes, if you like,' he said. 'It's a question of how you interpret it. Inflate the price or increase your profit. Yes.'

And we asked again for confirmation:

> 'But you weren't getting any more profit because you were only getting the price you'd already quoted?'
> 'Yes,' he replied, 'that is correct.'

There was no question that the original price, £41,750, included profit. The £18,000 was an inflation of the whole job, and the grant came in at 75 per cent of it. This was enough to cover the total actual cost, even though Stockport were required to meet a quarter of the cost. They even received £3,000 extra, then paid Ratcliffe £18,000, which he was required to pay straight back to them. He was, he said, 'quite angry and upset' about the affair.

This is not the image of the 'friendly club' that Stockport have sought to portray under Elwood's chairmanship, differentiating themselves from the Manchester clubs that have become corporations (one more successful than the other perhaps) through England's 1990s football boom. On the field, Danny Bergara had coached, cajoled and crafted his ragbag collection of signings into a serious lower division force, although the four Wembley disappointments, in 1992 and 1993, may have suggested he had taken them as far as he could.

He had, though, salvaged the self-respect of Stockport County and its fans. One lifelong fan told *On The Line*: 'He is a hero of mine. There are people here who would give their right arm to save Danny. He was held in such high esteem by a lot of people here.'

But not, ultimately, by the people with most reason to thank him – the chairman and directors. By 1995, Bergara, according to his contractual entitlements, was being paid close to £90,000 a year. He still lived near Sheffield and so had agreed with the club that he could stay in modest digs near Edgeley Park on odd late working nights. The club made available an accommodation allowance of £50 per week. As an arrangement for a successful football manager it was painfully unextravagant. In March 1995 Bergara agreed with Brendan Elwood that at the end of the season they would review the accommodation allowance.

Shortly afterwards, on 16 March, Stockport had a board meeting. Bergara was not there. He had asked if he could be excused from it and asked the chief executive, David Coxon, to speak on his behalf about playing matters. At that meeting, Elwood told the board, falsely, that Bergara had agreed that his £50 weekly accommodation allowance would 'cease forthwith'. Quite apart from the fact that this was untrue, nobody, according to Bergara, communicated this to him. Two weeks later he put in an expenses claim for the heartbreakingly petty sum of £64 with no idea that he was about to lose the job at which he had toiled for two decades.

The romantic involvement of the man from Uruguay with the club down the A6 ended in a foul split, an industrial tribunal hearing and a subsequent appeal, both of which Bergara won. After hearing the evidence, the tribunals reached their conclusions about what had happened. The club refused to pay the expenses claim, and Bergara lost his temper. He was abusive to Coxon and said that Elwood and David Jolley, the finance director, were 'bastards' for withholding his expenses. He referred to the two directors 'again in bad language' when speaking to his two deputies, John Sainty and Dave Jones. (Jones subsequently replaced Bergara as manager on a third of his salary.) The club's vice-chairman, Graham White, testified that when he met Bergara at a sponsors' dinner he heard him describing the chairman and finance director as 'fucking gangsters'.

Bergara accepted the tribunal's judgement that the swearing was 'out of order' and said that if he had been given the opportunity he would have apologized for it. But he had not been given the chance. However, the tribunal found that at the sponsors' dinner, at the Alma Lodge Hotel in the leafy Cheshire suburb of Altrincham, Bergara had behaved 'quite properly' in spite of statements to the contrary put forward by witnesses for the club. But Elwood did not do the same in the foyer after dinner: 'He swore at Mr Bergara, he sought to assault him by striking at him on two occasions and told him not to bother to turn up for work as he no longer had a job.'

The record of finance director David Jolley's behaviour was equally damning:

> [He] poked [Mr Bergara] in the chest and issued him with a tirade of swearing and abuse which he, Mr Jolley, described as a 'Sheffield volley' and then Mr Jolley said that (Bergara) was to come to a meeting at his office the following day and at that meeting he would 'tear up his contract and shove it up his arse'.

The tribunal further noted that 'It is suggested on behalf of the club that that was a very proper invitation to a disciplinary committee at which these matters would be fairly heard,' but dismissed this explanation. Had the consequences not been so serious for Bergara, the whole shabby story would have had its comic elements.

On 31 March Elwood told a board meeting that Bergara had assaulted him. The tribunal came to the opposite conclusion, but the story that Danny Bergara had hit his chairman went round the footballing world like wildfire and is the single biggest reason why Bergara has struggled to find another manager's job ever since. Here is a coach with rich experience, who who has spent most of that time underemployed at home near Sheffield. Yet the tribunal was unequivocal about what has since been accepted as a true piece of football gossip: 'That was clearly an untruth. It was Mr Elwood who tried to assault Mr Bergara.'

Acting on Elwood's version of events, which followed Elwood misleading the board about Bergara's expenses, the board voted to sack Danny summarily. In the end the industrial tribunal judged Bergara to have been 25 per cent to blame, for his 'intemperate, derogatory and vulgar remarks' and for not attending the meeting at which Jolley had promised to 'tear up his contract and shove it up his arse'. This meant that they considered the club to be 75 per cent to blame, declaring them to be 'an employer who, so far from being reasonable, had treated this employee, this manager, with a complete lack of frankness, in a disingenuous way, which must have been exceedingly provocative to him'.

Bergara won his case, and was paid damages, but not until August 1997 – nearly two and a half years later. When *On The Line* saw him, he declined to talk about it; the papers were there to see, he had won, he had nothing further to say. He talked only about football, about his record at Stockport and his work on the technique of the raw players he had brought to Edgeley Park, whom the club had sold on as lower division stars.

Bergara was a kid from a footballing family and his career began with Racing Club of Uruguay, then continued in Spain with Real Mallorca, where his coach was Cesar Rodrigues, his first mentor. He also met his wife, Janet, there, in Mallorca; she is English and was working in the travel industry. His next club was Seville, in the Spanish First Division, and he played against Barcelona and the Real Madrid of Puskas, di Stefano and Santamaria.

Sitting in his living room, frustrated, he came alive talking football. He had to quit playing because of injury and he and his wife decided to move to England. When he arrived in 1973 he could speak little English but a cousin of Janet's introduced him to Harry Haslam, who was then managing Luton Town. From this fragile link, Bergara carved out a career that touched many people, like Ricky Hill, the graceful Luton Town and England midfielder, who says he has Bergara to thank for making him a player. A career great in its unique way. And it all effectively ended with a seedy piece of outmanoeuvring over £64 living expenses, an attempted assault by Elwood and chest-poking and foul abuse from Jolley.

One close friend of Bergara's told *On The Line* that she laughed ruefully even at the 25 per cent fault attributed to him for the intemperate remarks made during the maelstrom:

Danny is a gentleman, a lovely man, totally opposite to the people running that club. The fact is that he had to learn to swear to fit in in English football, which is a crude and brutal place to work. It was just so laughable that he ends up being criticized for a way of behaving and language that, as a foreigner, he was taught by the English.

We learned that Bergara was not the only Stockport employee who had felt the need to make a claim to an industrial tribunal for unfair dismissal. Three others, accounts assistant Lyn Porter, lottery manager Tony Constance and safety officer Philip Collister, brought cases to the tribunal and had them settled by the club. Four instances in five years for a club that employed fewer than 20 non-playing staff is a record that David Cockburn, a solicitor and vice-president of the Employment Lawyers Association, told us indicated a nasty regime at the 'friendly club':

> I'd say that is a high number but it's not only a high number. I think it discloses an approach to a style of management which has little to do with modern management techniques. It's more a macho management where they will hire and fire at will, where they think they can develop more obedience than team spirit.

David Jolley has since left Stockport County but Brendan Elwood is still there, still chairman. His company, City Estates in Sheffield, was paid huge amounts of money by Stockport for 'construction and repair work for the ground and restaurant', £384,538 in 1998 and £612,715 in 1999. The club's accounts for 1999 show them owing City Estates a total of £1.2 million. There is nothing illegal with a club doing business with its chairman or a director, especially if no public money is involved, but *On The Line* asked Stockport what work was done for figures on such a scale. They replied:

> The figures referred to are totally inaccurate. The chairman's company has undertaken work for

Stockport County purely to finance projects. All transactions are done at arm's length and are correctly reported as related party transactions in the club's accounts. The chairman has a substantial amount invested in the football club which is completely interest free.

The club did not explain what the projects were.

We broadcast our findings about Stockport County's breaches of the Football Trust's rules on Radio 5 in August 2000, then immediately passed our file to the Trust and to the Football Association, which, as the game's governing body, has a responsibility to investigate. The FA announced it was formally investigating Stockport in January 2001 but since then very little has been heard. In September 2002, more than two years after the serious findings we broadcast, the Football Trust (now renamed the Football Foundation) told us: 'Stockport is on the FA's desk awaiting their decision to charge or not to charge.'

The FA told us: 'The investigation has still not concluded. We have had some new arrivals into the organization. It is not too far from a conclusion now, so it's a question of watch this space.' The FA has consistently insisted that it is committed to upholding its laws and clamping down on wrongdoing by football clubs. In the case of Stockport County, Greater Manchester's 'friendly club', it has been a long wait to see if the governing body will be true to their word.

CHAPTER EIGHT

Heading for Injury Time?
The Link Between Football and Alzheimer's Disease

In April 1999, the former Celtic player Billy McPhail had his day in court. The 70-year-old Glaswegian was a sad and confused figure as he sat in among the austere finery of Scotland's legal best. Certainly, a far cry from the day in 1957 when he propelled himself into the green-and-white side of the city's pantheon of heroes by heading three goals past Rangers in Celtic's record 7-1 League Cup final victory.

McPhail has been suffering from the symptoms of pre-senile dementia for almost a decade. He and his family were convinced that in his 17-year career as a professional footballer, the frequent impacts caused by heading a heavy leather ball contributed to his degenerative mental illness. McPhail's lawyers were arguing that he should be entitled to a £70 a week disability payment under the terms of the industrial injuries act.

They are still arguing. Two courts have thrown the case out and it is now wending its way to the nation's supreme legal chamber, the Court of Session.

McPhail is not the first footballer to try and prove that the wear-and-tear of professional football has left him crippled and that his ailments, for the purposes of welfare benefits and compensation, should be classified as industrial injuries. There is a growing case-load of more than 60 former footballers with damaged knees, hips, and feet battling the point against a determined government. But his case highlighted a peculiar phenomenon; that of growing numbers of post-war footballers suffering from dementia in general and Alzheimer's disease in particular, whose doctors and lawyers were making the case that the illness had been triggered by years of heading footballs.

Some of football's most dramatic goals have come from headers and one of the iconic images of the English game in particular has been the strapping lad at the back repelling all comers with the flat of his forehead. The suggestion that hefty and frequent contact between a head and an object travelling at some lick would have a detrimental impact on that most sophisticated and delicate of organs, the brain, was never considered a serious proposition.

Irish international Johnny Carey was one of the game's greats. He captained Manchester United just after the war leading the 'Reds' to FA Cup glory in 1948 and following that triumph with the league title in 1952. United boss Matt Busby regarded him as a natural leader and forceful personality who could play in any position. Today Carey's widow, Margaret, lives quietly in a modern sheltered flat in leafy Cheshire. She likes to remember her husband when he was young and full of life.

'I used to go dancing with my friends on a Saturday evening at Chorlton Baths in Chorlton cum Hardy, so he danced with me and said, "Where shall we meet on Tuesday evening?" Just like that. I had never met him before, so I said you must be joking. Anyway I rather fancied him, so I did. I went out with him. He was only 19 at the time and was the nicest person you could wish to meet. I never heard him say anything nasty about anyone and it was the same when he got Alzheimer's. A lot of Alzheimer sufferers are difficult, he was not. He was so lovely all the time.'

It was in 1990 that Johnny Carey showed the first signs of the debilitating illness from which he would suffer for the rest of his life. 'He started to worry about silly things,' Margaret recalls, 'nothing to really worry about.

Little things like driving the car. In fact, I had to stop him driving and that was the hardest thing I ever did.'

Soon Carey started to deteriorate even further. He took to wandering off in the middle of night and getting lost. On one occasion Margaret had to get the police to track him down. It soon became clear he could no longer stay at home and he was moved into a nursing home.

Carey died in 1995. But by then the death of an even more famous figure with Alzheimer's, the former Manchester City and England manager Joe Mercer, had led a Liverpool GP to launch an investigation into the prevalence of the disease among footballers.

John Rowlands is a doctor at a family health centre at Maghull, a suburb of Liverpool. 'My main interest in a possible link between dementia and professional football started in the late 1980s when my friend Joe Mercer became ill. Then, just about the time Joe passed away, his wife Nora found herself going to the funerals of other famous footballers of the same age. And she discovered that more and more of them had suffered from dementia and possibly Alzheimer's disease. It was from that, that we began to wonder if there could be, in fact, a problem with this group of professional people.'

Geoff Twentyman is another friend of Dr Rowlands and a former player who is suffering from Alzheimer's. Twentyman, who played at Anfield in the fifties, wound up being chief scout for Liverpool when he retired as a player. He sits at home in a suburban Merseyside semi. He goes out for a walk most afternoons, not always finding his own way back. Physically he looks fine and is active, but it is clear he struggles to concentrate. 'I think it is the worst thing I have ever had in my life and I have had a lot of complaints, but this Alzinas...' His voice trails off.

Geoff's fading memories are preserved for his wife Pat in the neat, hand-written scouting log he kept on his travels. In it can be seen the initial notes on prospects over whom Geoff had cast his expert eyes years ago. Players like Phil Neal.

Phil Neal ... done well, good prospect, satisfactory game, worth a follow up.

Elsewhere in the book there are reports on John Toshack, Kevin Keegan, Ray Clemence – and even ones that got away like Francis Lee.

Pat recalls that when Geoff first started to suffer from Alzheimer's most people thought he had been hitting the bottle. 'A few people said they thought he was drinking too much, but he wasn't. It was just that he was confused.'

And that is the tragedy of Alzheimer's and other forms of dementia. Sufferers gradually descend into a twilight world of confusion.

'Time means nothing to Geoff, you know what I mean? He can get up at three am, and have a shower and a shave thinking it is time to get up. He will wake up in the middle of the night and ask "Who are you?" We have been married 46 years and he is asking me who I am.'

Dr Rowlands sent Geoff to see consultant neurologist Mark Doran at the Walton Centre in Liverpool, which pecializes in head injuries, and attached a note asking if he had noticed a higher-than-average incidence of dementia in former footballers. Doran was intrigued. Together they drew up plans to track down as many former professional footballers as they could between the ages of 55 and 70, their plans given an impetus by news of the death of Bob Paisley, one of the most successful managers in English footballing history.

Paisley, who passed away in 1996, had succumbed to Alzheimer's at the beginning of the 1990s around the same time as Johnny Carey. But Bob Paisley, Joe Mercer and Johnny Carey were not the only famous footballers to die with the disease. Another was Spurs' great Danny Blanchflower and more recently the England manager Alf Ramsey. In fact, the Liverpool doctors tracked down around 35 footballers in their target range who had suffered from Alzheimer's or a similar condition. They also discovered they were not alone in their thoughts.

In 1989 tests on 69 players in Norway had discovered disturbances on their brain scans most likely due to neuronal damage caused by repeated minor head traumas. A couple of years later, the same Oslo scientists put 37 former Norwegian internationals through a battery of psychological tests. This time they discovered, '...mild-to-severe deficits of attention, concentration, memory and judgement in 81 per cent of the players. This may indicate some degree of permanent organic brain damage, probably the cumulative result of repeated traumas from heading the ball. We must conclude that blows to the head by heading show convincing evidence of brain damage similar to that found in patients who have sustained minor head injuries'.

Still more research, this time conducted in the United States in 1995, found that players who usually headed the ball ten times or more in a game had lower average IQs than team mates who headed the ball less frequently. They also did less well in tests assessing attention span, mental flexibility, facial recognition and visual searching.

More recently in 1997, Dutch neurologists focused on 53 professional footballers from a number of clubs in the Dutch league. They compared them to 27 élite athletes in non-contact sports. Both groups were subjected to a series of tests. The results showed players exhibited impaired performances in memory, planning and visual perception when compared to the non-contact sport performers.

According to the study, a player who takes part in 300 league games in a career will head the ball 2,000 times at speeds anywhere up to 100 miles an hour. The study concluded that, although heading the ball was a lot less traumatic than blows received by a boxer for example, the relationship between brain injury and heading the ball was a matter of public concern.

Under the rules of the game a football should weigh between 16 and 14 ounces. Although there has been much comment during recent World Cups about wayward shots being the result of a new lighter ball being used for international competition, this is a fallacy. The weight of a football before the game starts has always been between 14 and 16 ounces. What has changed has been the materials used to make the ball. Modern materials could conceivably cause less friction, meaning the ball will travel further for the same effort, but what is undoubtedly true is that the old leather ball absorbed water and got considerably heavier as the match progressed, anything up to 20 per cent heavier.

Still, even the waterproofed modern ball can pack some punch. The fastest shot recorded in the Premier League was by David Beckham in a match against Chelsea in 1997. It was tracked at 97.9 miles an hour. At the University of Manchester Institute of Science and Technology (UMIST) Professor Steve Ried has created a test to measure the impact of leather on skull.

'What we decided to do was to see whether we could quantify the effect of the impact of a ball on the speed with which the head recoils on impact. There is a standard scientific index for this, believe it or not, called the Gadd Severity Index.'

The Gadd Severity Index is generally used to help develop safety features in cars and such like. An index reading of 1000 would cause severe concussion in a normal healthy adult. Professor Reid's test showed that had a head interrupted Beckham's shot it would have generated a reading of 300.

'The effect of any impact on the head is to generate shock-waves within the skull and within the brain. And these waves compress the brain. They compress the material and cause it to deform and then, when they have travelled through and reached a free surface at the back of the head, they are then reflected back causing tension within the brain.'

A glancing blow from a mistimed header could cause even more danger.

'It would complicate the problem because that would simply cause the head to rotate so that, instead of simply having compression and tension in the brain and between the brain and the skull, you could generate perhaps quite high-shear defamation there which might tear the ligaments and the connection between the brain and the skull causing a different kind of injury. Basically when you send stress waves through any material you deform them; and if you deform them rapidly and regularly you produce damage – and that damage can become permanent.'

By the mid 1990s the mounting evidence from Europe and the United States indicated the possibility of a problem, and it did not seem to matter whether people played with the old leather ball prone to becoming water-logged or its modern equivalent. The Liverpool doctors planned a campaign called Neuro 96 coinciding with the

Euro 96 football championship to raise a quarter of a million pounds for further research.

Mike Doran recalls, 'We have had promises of money, but nothing has materialized. To a degree, I am a bit surprised about this because I would have thought the research is in the interest of both the population at large and, more specifically, to those people who play football.'

Even when John Rowlands wrote to four Premiership clubs, asking for help, he got no joy. One club told him it was a matter for the Professional Footballers Association.

'I was a little bit surprised by that – the feeling that, without considering the cost, it should be the players themselves who needed to look into the research. So that was sort of the employees being told they have to look after their own health.'

Rowlands next port of call was the PFA. 'They were much more sympathetic and helpful, at least up to a point. They said they would support us with up to half the cost of the research but that we would have to go elsewhere for the rest. Unfortunately that proved very difficult. I contacted some drug companies but got no joy, and basically I am still looking.'

There was no Neuro 96. At the Professional Footballers Association HQ in Manchester, chairman Gordon Taylor has a bulging file of reports and correspondence relating to this topic. He says players feel the risk from heading the ball is so slight that in the past the PFA did not feel it worthwhile to stump up all the cash for a proper study, although the money is still on the table.

'We would be prepared to play a part in funding research to try to make it clear once and for all whether this is a fact or just a possibility. In an ideal world, it would be nice to know exactly what the consequences are of everything we do, so that we could all weigh up the risk.'

The truth is that establishing a definite link between heading a ball and Alzheimer's would not be welcome news to professional football. And whenever the matter is even hinted at in the press, football responds with maximum scorn. Take Bobby Gould's reaction to the report by the American study in 1995 that soccer players were more susceptible to brain damage than American football players.

'When you look at all the great headers of the ball back in the old days they aren't brain damaged, so it is hardly likely the players these days will be injured.'

That, as we know, is simply not true, but this comment was followed up by the FA who issued a statement in the wake of the American research stating, 'There is no evidence that any player in this country has ever received head injuries from heading the ball'.

Heading the ball is undoubtedly an integral part of the game and for those who might want to ban it, it can be pointed out that people indulge in all sorts of sport – most obviously boxing – where the danger is considerably greater than anything generated in football. As Gordon Taylor puts it, 'It's a delicate problem' – delicate because if the clubs know about it but do not inform their players of the possibility they could lay themselves open to legal action.

There is another factor to take into account, this is the recent discovery of a gene which may help identify people at greater risk of dementia. Harry Cayton is the executive director of the Alzheimer Disease Society. 'Everyone inherits genes from their parents and there is a protein called Alipoprotein E, or Apo-E for short, which occurs in all human cells. We all have it but it occurs in three different forms, a bit like blood groups and if you have the

Apo-E 4 gene, that appears to increase your risk of developing Alzheimer's later in life. If you carry the Apo-E 2 gene, that appears to inhibit the development of Alzheimer's. So the research suggests, for example, that if you have the Apo-E 4 gene, you are seven times more likely to develop Alzheimer's in later life than if you have the Apo-E 2.'

One in 25 people may have the Apo-E 4 gene. Peter Hamlyn, the London surgeon who saved the life of the boxer Michael Watson, says a simple genetic test would uncover those who may be at risk.

'With that information you could then give advice as to whether a career in contact sports was a sensible option, or at least inform people of the risk. I do not think you should go and screen a large number of professional sportsmen and tell them to give up. You can simply make the test available to young men and women who are in their teens and starting to develop an interest in contact sports. You might see clubs – before they take on juniors – screen them for this sort of thing. I would have thought that once parents know about this sort of thing, they will be very keen on it.'

The Football Association, now no longer so dismissive of the notion, has its own brain expert, the eminent neurologist Myles Gibson from Leeds. He feels that a survey of past footballers is of little use, but says there is probably a need to study current and aspirant professionals.

'We have studied the reports very carefully as they have come out and, although you can pick out scientific flaws in them from a scientific point of view, I have little doubt that this is something we have got to look at. But the difficulty is how to get the numbers right, how to get the correct aggregation of people so you can definitely say that, yes, footballers get Alzheimer's more commonly than the rest of the population.'

He does admit, however, that, in any other walk of life, he would not advise a young man to take up a job which requires him being repeatedly hit on the head for several months of the year. Like Harry Cayton he believes a profitable line of research would be to develop a test to screen for Apo-E 4.

'When you consider that just a few years ago we were not very knowledgeable about cardiac problems, but now we are in a position to test for heart problems and give very clear advice to youngsters, then the same may soon be the case in relation to the head.'

Should such a test become widely available – as seems likely in the none too distant future – then football clubs may well be forced to use it if they want their players to be insured. Football, in the past, has often behaved as if it were outside the law. The Bosman case was an excellent example of the game waking up to the fact that it is not. Likewise, as Duncan Ferguson discovered to his cost, a head- butt on the pitch, in the eyes of the law, is the same thing as a head-butt on a street corner. Thus proving a link between heading the ball and Alzheimer's could have massive legal implications.

Anthony Coombs is a Manchester solicitor who specializes in injury at work. 'It raises the possibility of future compensation claims by players against their clubs or possibly even the governing body which makes the rules. What you would have to show is that the club, or whoever, showed a lack of initiative in finding out something which in itself is not obvious. On this point a judge once ruled that "The employer must keep up to date but the court will be slow to blame him for not ploughing a lone furrow". It will depend a lot on the resources and wealth of the employer, but obviously football clubs are not poor.'

If this all sounds theoretical twaddle then consider the story of asbestos. At one time this was thought to be a harmless dust, but after it was discovered to be a killer. It was responsible for a series of worldwide insurance claims that led Lloyds of London and their 'names' to the brink of ruin in the late 1980s and early 1990s.

Much of the debate about Alzheimer's, needless to say, has passed the vast majority of professional footballers by. This means that players like recently retired Gary Mabutt, for example, live with a risk they know little or nothing about.

'I have spent most of my career as a centre-half and that, of course, is probably the position where you are heading the ball the most.'

Mabutt was concerned when he saw the evidence about the link between heading the ball and Alzheimer's, but is wary of over-reaction: 'Anything that can be detrimental to a professional footballer – or to anybody playing football – needs to be investigated, but basically players will consider that you get all sorts of injuries in football. We all know old footballers who have knackered knees or hips, but we are prepared to live with the risks because we love the game.'

There is no proven link between Alzheimer's and football, but then there has been precious little research into such a link, a point acknowledged by medical experts called by the Government opposing Billy McPhail's disability claim. What is clear is that there is an accumulation of anecdotal evidence, and evidence from small-scale scientific studies around the world, and that medical men involved with football no longer laugh at the suggestion that a key part of the game of football can cause brain damage.

The potential for legal action in the future means

clubs and the game's governing bodies may not be as willing to live with the risks as most players undoubtedly would. The FA says that it is currently conducting an audit of injuries in the professional game. This is, it says, just the start of long-term research which will eventually help it to assess the effects that heading a ball has on the brain.

If it is found to be unacceptably dangerous, could it lead to headers being banned?

The FA's medical man, Myles Gibson, says it will certainly open a tortured debate. 'You can just imagine the sort of debate that would take place in the chambers of football if we come up with medical evidence that could force a change in the way in which football is played.'

Dr David Kernick, club doctor with Exeter City, has carried out a peer review of evidence so far and, like the FA's man, Myles Gibson, believes it is time for the footballing authorities to pull their finger out and pay for credible research.

He says, 'One of the problems with much of the research that has been carried out is that it has compared footballers with other sportsmen. Now, it is unfortunately true that many footballers do hit the bottle once they have retired and, as alcohol abuse is also a major trigger for dementia, it is possible that this rather than heading the ball has led to this seeming connection. Perhaps more definitive research could be obtained if, for example, goalkeepers were compared with central defenders.'

The immediate action for football should be to move quickly to discover if heading does trigger Alzheimer's in sufficient numbers to justify genuine concern. After all, we are talking about the biggest and richest sport in the world and such medical research as there has been, suggests that it is worth a serious look.